Josiah Hughes

Hughes's common school branches in a nutshell

Josiah Hughes

Hughes's common school branches in a nutshell

ISBN/EAN: 9783337727307

Printed in Europe, USA, Canada, Australia, Japan

Cover: Foto ©ninafisch / pixelio.de

More available books at **www.hansebooks.com**

HUGHES'

COMMON SCHOOL BRANCHES

IN A NUTSHELL.

PREPARED FOR THE BENEFIT OF TEACHERS AND STUDENTS.

BY JOSIAH HUGHES,

Author of "The Teachers' and Students' Question Book" and "Questions and Answers on U. S. History."

PUBLISHED BY THE AUTHOR, CHARLESTON, W. VA.

CHARLESTON, W. VA.:
BUTLER PRINTING COMPANY,
1893

PREFACE.

The object aimed at in the preparation of this work has been to compile a pocket library of the branches taught in the Common Schools, for the use of teachers, advanced students and private learners in reviewing the branches, and extending their knowledge of them.

In every branch of study there are certain essential principles and facts which should be remembered. These should be reviewed frequently, for every repetition seems to impress an object of thought more indelibly upon the memory. The review should not be voluminous, yet it should be comprehensive enough to give the student a clear knowledge of the subject reviewed. In the preparation of this work, the author's aim has been to furnish just such a review.

The author submits this work to a discriminating public, with the hope that it may prove to be helpful to teachers and students.

INDEX.

ORTHOGRAPHY	5
READING	9
PENMANSHIP	12
U. S. HISTORY	15
GEOGRAPHY	27
PHYSIOLOGY	35
CIVIL GOVERNMENT	41
BOOK-KEEPING	48
TEACHING	52
GRAMMAR	57
ARITHMETIC	79
GENERAL HISTORY	93

Orthography.

1. **Orthography** treats of lettters, syllables, and words.

2. **A Letter** is a character used to represent one or more elementary sounds.

3. **An Alphabet** is a system of characters used to represent the elementary sounds of a language.

4. **The name** of a letter is the appellation by which it is known.

5. **The Power** of a letter is the elementary sound which it represents.

6. Letters are **divided**, with respect to the sounds they represent, into **Vowels and Consonants**.

7. **A Vowel** is a letter that stands for a free, open sound of the voice.

8. **A Consonant** is a letter that stands for a sound made by the obstructed voice or the obstructed breath.

9. **The Vowels** are *a, e, i, o, u, w*, and *y*.

10. *W* and *y* are consonants, when they immediately precede a vowel sounded in the same syllable.

11. **The Vowel Sounds** of *w* and *y* are the same as those of *u* and *i*.

12. **I** is a consonant, when it represents the sound of *y* consonant.

13. **U** is a consonant, when it has the sound of *w* consonant.

14. **A, e,** and **o** are always vowels.

15. **A Diphthong** is the union of two vowels in one sound.

16. **A Proper Diphthong** is one in which both vowels are sounded.

17. **An Improper Diphthong,** or *digraph*, is one in which but one vowel is sounded.

18. **A Triphthong,** or *trigraph*, is the union of three vowels in the same *syllable*.

19. **Consonants Classified:** (1.) As to the nature of the sound represented, consonants may be classified as *Subvocals* and *Aspirates*. (2.) As to position of organs in giving the sounds, they may be classified as *Mutes* and *Semivowels*. (3.) As to the organs that mainly operate to produce consonant sounds, they may be classified as *Labials, Linguals, Linguo-dentals, Linguo-nasals, Palato-nasals* and *Palatals*.

20. **Subvocals** are those consonants which represent subvocal or obstructed sounds.

21. **Aspirates** are those consonants which represent *sharp, hissing* sounds.

22. **Mutes** are those consonants whose sounds can not be prolonged.

23. **Semivowels** are those consonants whose sounds may be prolonged.

24. **Labials** are letters whose sounds are made by the lips.

25. **Linguals** are letters whose sounds are made by the tongue.

26. **Linguo-dentals** are letters whose sounds are made by the tongue and teeth.

ORTHOGRAPHY.

27. **Linguo-nasals** are letters whose sounds are articulated by the tongue, the sound passing through the nose.

28. **Palato-nasals** are letters whose sounds are made by the palate, the sound passing through the nose.

29. **Liquids** are those letters which represent sounds which seem to flow readily into other sounds. They are *l, m, n,* and *r.*

30. **Redundant Letters** are those which have no sounds of their own; as, *c, x. q, j.*

31. **Cognate Letters** are those whose sounds are produced by the same organs of speech in a similar manner, as *f* and *v.*

32. **A Final Letter** is one that ends a word.

33. **A Silent Letter** is one not sounded.

34. **An Aphthong** is a silent letter.

35. **An Elementary Sound** is a simple sound.

36. **The Elementary Sounds** of the English language are divided into *Vocals, Subvocals,* and *Aspirates.*

REMARK.—Mark the distinction between subvocal *sounds* and subvocal *letters;* also between *aspirate* sounds and *aspirate* letters.

37. **A Syllable** is a letter, or a combination of letters, uttered with one impulse of the voice.

38. **A Word** is a syllable, or a combination of syllables, used as the sign of an idea.

39. **Accent** is a stress of voice laid on a certain syllable when a word is uttered.

40. With respect to their number of syllables, words are divided into four classes; *Monosyllables, Dissyllables, Trisyllables,* and *Polysyllables.*

41. **A Monosyllable** is a word of one syllable.

42. **A Dissyllable** is a word of two syllables.

43. A **Trisyllable** is a word of three syllables.
44. A **Polysyllable** is a word of four or more syllables.
45. With respect to their form, words are classified as *Primitive, Derivative,* and *Compound.*
46. A **Primitive Word** is one which is not derived from any other in the same language.
47. A **Derivative Word** is one which is formed from a single simpler word, by the addition of one or more letters.
48. A **Compound Word** is one composed of two or more words.
49. A **Prefix** is an addition to the beginning of a word.
50. A **Suffix** is an addition to the end of a word.
51. The **Root** of a derivative word is the primitive part.
52. The **Base** of a compound word is the part modified.
53. **Syllabication** is the proper division of words into syllables.
54. The **Ultimate Syllable** is the last syllable of a word.
55. The **Penultimate Syllable** is the last but one.
56. The **Antepenultimate Syllable** is the last but two.
57. The **Preantepenultimate Syllable** is the last but three.
58. The **Basis** of a written or printed syllable is the *vowel.*
59. The **Basis** of a spoken syllable is the *vocal.*
60. **Orthoepy** treats of the correct pronunciation of **words.**

61. **Phonology** treats of the science of elementary sounds.

62. **Diacritical Marks** are characters used to indicate the sounds of letters.

63. **Spelling** is the distinct expression of the letters or sounds of a word, in their proper order.

64. **Orthographic Spelling** is the expression of the *letters* of a word, in their proper order.

65. **Phonetic Spelling** is the expression of the *elementary sounds* of a word, in their proper order.

66. **Pronunciation** is the act of uttering words or parts of words.

Reading.

1. **Reading** is imbibing the thoughts, feelings, and sentiments of an author.

2. **Silent Reading** is imbibing the thoughts, feelings, and sentiments of an author, without giving utterance to the language.

3. **Audible Reading** is imbibing the thoughts, feelings, and sentiments of an author, and giving utterance to the language.

4. **Elocution** is the science and art of the delivery of composition.

5. **Articulation** is the distinct utterance of the elementary sounds, and of their combinations in words.

6. **Emphasis** is a stress of voice placed on one or more words of a sentence.

7. **Absolute Emphasis** is that which is independent of any contrast or comparison with other words or ideas.

8. **Antithetic Emphasis** (*Relative*) is that which is used where there is antithesis either expressed or implied.

9. **Cumulative Emphasis** is that which is applied to a succession of emphatic words in which the last receives more emphasis than the one preceding it.

10. **Inflections** are slides of the voice either upward or downward.

11. **The Rising Inflection** is that in which the voice slides *upward*.

12. **The Falling Inflection** is that in which the voice slides *downward*.

13. **The Circumflex** is a union of the rising and falling inflections on the same word.

14. **Modulation** is the correct variations of the voice in reading and speaking.

15. **Monotone** is an unvaried tone throughout a sentence or discourse.

16. **Cadence** is the natural dropping of the voice at the close of a sentence.

17. **Pauses** are cessations of the voice in reading and speaking.

18. **The Grammatical Pauses** are those which indicate the grammatical divisions of discourse. They are represented by the punctuation marks.

19. **The Rhetorical Pauses** are those made in order to bring out the sense or express the sentiment They are not marked, but are determined wholly by the sense to be expressed and the judgment of the reader.

20. **Quantity** has reference to *loudness* or *volume* of sound.

21. **Force** is the degree of loudness or energy with which sounds are uttered.

22. **Stress** is force applied to particular parts of monosyllabic words or syllables.

23. **Slur** is that smooth, gliding, subdued movement of the voice applied to the less important parts of a discourse.

24. **Quality** has reference to the kind of tone used in speaking and reading.

25. **Pitch** refers to the general tone of the voice in reading and speaking.

26. **The Key-Note** is the standard pitch of the voice in reading and speaking.

27. **The Compass** of the voice is its general range above and below the *key-note*.

28. **Rate** is the degree of rapidity with which the voice moves in reading and speaking.

29. **Gesture** refers to the movements of the body and its members.

30. **Transition** is change in the manner of expression.

31. **Personation** is the representation of the tones and manners of other persons.

32. **A Series** is a number of particulars following one another in the same construction.

33. **A Climax** is a series of particulars gradually increasing in importance to the last.

Penmanship.

1. **Penmanship** is the art of writing. It is based upon movement.
2. **Movement** is the manner of moving the arm, hand, and pen in writing.
3. **Kinds of Movement:** Finger, Fore-arm (Muscular), Combined, and Whole Arm.
4. **The Finger Movement** is that in which the arm and hand rest and the fingers and thumb contract.
5. **The Fore-arm Movement** (Muscular) is the action of the fore-arm upon its muscular rest below the elbow, keeping the first and second fingers from motion.
6. **The Combined Movement** is the united action of the fore-arm and the first and second fingers.
7. **The Whole Arm Movement** is that in which the arm moves independent of any muscular rest.
8. **Position** relates to the manner of sitting at the desk. The principal positions used in writing are the Front, the Right, and the Left positions.
9. **A Line** is the path of a moving pen.
10. **A Straight Line** is one which has no change of direction.
11. **A Curved Line** is one which has a continuous change of direction. There are two kinds of curved lines,—*right curve* and *left curve*.
12. **A Right Curve** is one which bends to the right of a straight line uniting its extremities.

13. A **Left Curve** is one which bends to the left of a straight line uniting its extremities.

14. **Parallel Lines** are lines which have the same direction, and are equally distant from each other throughout their entire length.

15. A **Horizontal Line** is one which is level, one end being no higher than the other.

16. A **Vertical Line** is one which leans neither to the right nor the left.

17. An **Angle** is the opening between two lines meeting in a point.

18. A **Point** is the beginning or ending of a line, or the angular joining of two lines.

19. A **Loop** is two crossing lines uniting at one end.

20. A **Turn** is the merging of one distinct line into another.

21. An **Oval** is an egg-shaped figure.

22. A **Direct Oval** is one which begins with a descending left curve.

23. A **Reversed Oval** is one which begins with an ascending left curve.

24. The **Base Line** is the one upon which the letters rest.

25. The **Head Line** is the one to which the short letters extend.

26. The **Intermediate Line** is the one to which the semi-extended letters extend.

27. The **Top Line** is the one to which the extended letters extend.

28. A **Space** in height is the vertical height of the small letter i.

29. A **Space** in width is the horizontal distance between the straight lines in the small letter u.

30. **Classification of Letters.**—The twenty-six letters have two distinct forms called Small and Capital. The capital letters are divided into three classes,—Direct Oval, Reversed Oval, and Capital Stem. The small letters are also divided into three classes,—Short, Semi-extended, and Extended.

31. **The Short Letters** are thirteen in number, and are one space in height, except r and s, which are one and one-fourth spaces. They are $i, u, w, n, m, v, x, o, c, a, e, r,$ and s.

32. **The Semi-extended Letters** are so called because, as to their length, they are between the short and the extended letters. They are $t, d, p,$ and q.

33. **The Extended Letters**, or *loop letters*, are those whose principal form is the extended loop. They are $h, k, l, b, j, y, g, f,$ and z.

34. **Slant** is the inclination of letters from a vertical position. The *degree* is the unit of measure. The *main slant* is 52 degrees, and the *connective slant* is 30 degrees.

35. **Principles** are the constituent parts of letters. Most authors give seven principles, viz: (1.) straight line. (2.) right curve, (3.) left curve, (4.) extended loop, (5.) direct oval, (6.) reversed oval, and (7.) capital stem.

36. **Pen Holding.**—Hold the pen between the first two fingers and the thumb, so that it will cross the second finger at the root of the nail, the first finger resting on the holder about one inch from the point of the pen. Place the thumb against the holder opposite the first joint of the first finger, the holder crossing this finger just in front of the knuckle joint. The third and fourth fingers should be brought back under the hand, and should slide freely on the paper.

U. S. History.

970. Greenland discovered by Gunbiorn, a Norwegian.

1001. Leif Erikson and Biorn, of Iceland, explored Vinland, Canada, Massachusetts, and other parts of North America.

1492. Columbus discovered America, at the island of Guanahani, one of the Bahamas.

1497. John Cabot discovered the coast of North America.

1498. South America discovered by Columbus.

1499. Amerigo Vespucci, an Italian, a native of Florence, visited America, drew a map of the country, and wrote letters giving an account of his discoveries. His letters were published by a German geographer, who named the country in honor of Vespucci.

1512. Ponce de Leon, a Spaniard, seeking for a fabled fountain of immortal youth, discovered Florida.

1513. Balboa, a Spaniard, discovered the Pacific Ocean.

1518. Grijalva, a Spaniard, explored the southern coast of Mexico.

1519-'21. Cortez, a Spaniard, conquered Mexico.

1520. Magellan, a Spaniard, discovered and sailed through the strait which bears his name, named the Pacific Ocean, and made the first circumnavigation of the globe.

1524. Verazzani, an Italian in the service of the

French government, explored the eastern coast of North America.

1528. Narvaez, a Spaniard, explored part of Florida.

1534–'35. Cartier, a Frenchman, explored and named the gulf and river of St. Lawrence.

1541. De Soto, a Spaniard, discovered the Mississippi River.

1565. Melendez, a Spaniard, founded St. Augustine, Florida; the first permanent settlement in the United States.

1576. Frobisher, an Englishman, attempted to find a north-west passage to Asia.

1579. Sir Francis Drake, an Englishman, explored the Pacific coast.

1582. Espejo, a Spaniard, explored New Mexico, and founded Santa Fe; the second oldest town in the United States.

1584. Raleigh, an Englishman, sent out an expedition to Roanoke Island.

1585. Lane's Colony, Raleigh's first attempt to form a settlement.

1587. White's Colony, Raleigh's second attempt.

1602. Gosnold, an Englishman, explored the coast of Massachusetts, and discovered and named Cape Cod.

1607. Jamestown settled; the first permanent English settlement in the United States.

1608. Champlain, a Frenchman, founded Quebec, and (1609.) discovered Lake Champlain.

1609. Henry Hudson, an Englishman in the service of the Dutch, discovered the Hudson River.

1614. Settlement of New York by the Dutch.

1619. First Legislative Assembly in America, at Jamestown, Virginia.

1620. Slavery first introduced by a sale of twenty Africans, made by the Dutch to the Georgetown, Virginia, planters.

1620. Pilgrim Fathers, or *Puritans*, settled at New Plymouth, Mass.; the first permanent English settlement in New England.

1630. Boston founded by John Winthrop.

1634. Maryland settled by the second Lord Baltimore.

1636. Rhode Island settled by Roger Williams.

1637. Pequod War. John Mason led the colonial army; the tribe perished in a day.

1643. Union of the New England Colonies,—Massachusetts Bay, Plymouth, Connecticut, and New Haven.

1651. Navigation Act passed; enforced in 1660, giving England entire control of all the trade of the colonies.

1664. New York taken by the English, and the present name given.

1673. New York re-gained by the Dutch, but lost again the next year.

1675. King Philip, son of Massasoit, made war on the New England settlers; King Philip, after losing most all his warriors by death, and his family by capture, fled to his home, where he was shot by a faithless Indian.

1676. Bacon's Rebellion. CAUSE: Governor Berkeley refused Bacon a commission to make war on hostile Indians, and Bacon went against them without any commission except his sword. Governor Berkeley declared him a rebel, and afterward refused him a commission, although the Indians were committing depredations every day. A rebellion followed. Bacon died of fever, and his death ended the rebellion.

1682. **William Penn**, an English Quaker, founded the colony of Pennsylvania as an asylum for the persecuted English Quakers.

1689-1697. **King William's War**, a war between England and France, which extended to their American colonies. Closed by the Treaty of Ryswick.

1692. **Salem Witchcraft**, a delusion which prevailed at Salem, Massachusetts. Twenty persons were hanged and many others were tortured into confession, and thus saved themselves from punishment.

1702-1713. **Queen Anne's War**, caused in Europe by an attempt made by England to prevent the union of France and Spain. In Europe it was called the War of the Spanish Succession. Closed by the Treaty of Utrecht.

1733. **Georgia** settled by James Oglethorpe, an Englishman, whose object was to found an asylum for the persecuted Protestants of Europe, and for the poor who were imprisoned for debt, and others imprisoned for crime.

1744-1748. **King George's War**, caused in Europe by disputes over the succession to the Austrian throne, in which France and England espoused opposite causes. The war extended to the French and English colonies in America. In Europe it was known as the War of the Austrian Succession. Closed by the Treaty of Aix-la-Chapelle.

1754-1763. **French and Indian War**, caused by the conflicting claims of England and France.

1755. **Braddock's Defeat** near Fort Du Quesne, now Pittsburgh.

1756. War formally declared by the French.

1759. **Capture of Quebec**; Wolfe and Montcalm, the commanders, killed.

1763. **Treaty of Paris**; France ceded to England all her North American possessions east of the Mississippi, except the island and city of New Orleans.

1765. The **Stamp Act** passed by Parliament.

1765. The **First Colonial Congress** met in New York.

1774. The **First Continental Congress** met in Philadelphia.

1775-1781. **Revolutionary War**, a war between England and her American colonies, caused mainly by an attempt made by England to tax the colonies, without allowing them representation in the British Parliament.

1775. Battle of **Lexington**, the first battle of the war.

1776. Declaration of Independence, July 4; proposed by Richard Henry Lee; prepared by Thomas Jefferson, John Adams, Benjamin Franklin, Roger Sherman, and Robert R. Livingston; written by Thomas Jefferson.

1777. Burgoyne surrendered his whole army to Gates, at Saratoga,—the turning event of the war.

1778. The **Treaty of Alliance** with France, by which France acknowledged the American Independence, and agreed to send a fleet of sixteen vessels and an army of 4,000 men to assist in the war.

1779. John Paul Jones, a Scotch-American, noted for his wonderful pluck and skill in war, captured the Serapis and the Countess.

1780. Arnold's Treason. He sought and obtained command of West Point, a very important fortress. He bargained with General Clinton to deliver up the fortress for a general's commission in the British army and ten thousand pounds sterling. Major Andre, Clinton's messenger, was captured, and Arnold fled to a British vessel. Andre was hanged as a spy, October 2.

1781. War ended by the surrender of Cornwallis to Washington, at Yorktown, October 19.

1782. John Adams, Benjamin Franklin, Henry Laurens, and John Jay were appointed commissioners to conclude a treaty with Great Britain. November 30, a preliminary treaty was signed at Paris.

1783. The final treaty of peace, the **Treaty of Paris,** signed, September 3, and the United States gained their independence.

1787. The Constitutional Convention met at Philadelphia to revise the Articles of Confederation, but finding them too weak and defective for revision, formed an entirely new constitution, which was adopted the same year, and submitted to the several States for their ratification.

1788. The Constitution ratified by all the States except Rhode Island and North Carolina.

1789. The First Congress under the new constitution met at New York; George Washington inaugurated; Hamilton, Jefferson, Knox, Randolph, and Jay appointed as members of the cabinet.

Washington, 1789-1797.

1791. Vermont admitted into the Union.
1792. Kentucky admitted into the Union.
1793. The cotton-gin invented by Eli Whitney.

1794. The Whiskey Insurrection in Western Pennsylvania.
1796. Tennessee admitted into the Union.

Adams, 1797-1801.
1797. Troubles with France.
1798. Alien and Sedition laws passed.
1799. Death of Washington at Mt. Vernon.
1800. Capital removed to Washington.

Jefferson, 1801-1809.
1802. Ohio admitted into the Union.
1803. Louisiana purchased from France for $15,000,000.
1804. Lewis and Clarke expedition; Hamilton-Burr duel.
1807. First steamboat on the Hudson, invented by Robert Fulton.
1807. Embargo law passed.

Madison, 1809-1817.
1811. General Harrison defeated the Indians at Tippecanoe.
1812. War declared against Great Britain, because of her violation of American commercial rights.
1812. Louisiana admitted into the Union.
1813. Perry's victory on Lake Erie.
1814. Treaty of Peace at Ghent, December 24.
1815. Battle of New Orleans, January 8.
1816. National Bank established by Congress.
1816. Indiana admitted into the Union.

Monroe, 1817-1825.
1817. Mississippi admitted into the Union.
1818. Illinois admitted into the Union.
1819. Alabama admitted into the Union.
1819. Florida purchased from Spain for $5,000,000.

1820. Missouri Compromise passed; Maine admitted.
1821. Missouri admitted into the Union.
1824. General Lafayette visited the United States.

John Quincy Adams. 1825-1829.

1826. John Adams and Thomas Jefferson died, July 4.
1826. The first railroad in the United States completed.
1828. Revision of the Tariff, the "American System."

Jackson. 1829-1837.

1831. James Monroe died, July 4.
1832. Nullification ordinance passed by South Carolina,
1832. Black Hawk War began.
1833. National Funds removed from the U. S. Bank.
1835. Seminole War begun by Osceola.
1836. Arkansas admitted into the Union.
1837. Michigan admitted into the Union.

Van Buren. 1837-1841.

1837. Great financial panic.
1838. Anti-slavery agitation.
1840. Sub-Treasury Bill passed.

W. H. Harrison, 1841.

1841. Harrison died one month after inauguration.

Tyler, 1841-1845.

1842. The Webster–Ashburton Treaty settled the dispute between the United States and Great Britain over the boundary line of Maine.
1842. Dorr's Rebellion in Rhode Island.

1843. The first magnetic telegraph erected in the world was put up between Washington and Baltimore.

1844. First public message sent was concerning Polk's nomination for the presidency.

1845. Florida and Texas admitted into the Union.

Polk, 1845-1849.

1846. Mexico declared war against the United States, caused by the annexation of Texas, which was claimed by Mexico.

1846. Iowa admitted into the Union.

1847. The city of Mexico surrendered.

1848. Treaty of Guadaloupe Hildalgo, by which the United States gained the territory now comprised in New Mexico, Utah, and California; and the Rio Grande for the western boundary of the disputed territory. Mexico received $18,250,000 as purchase money.

1848. Gold discovered in California.

1848. Wisconsin admitted into the Union.

Taylor, 1849-1850.

1850. Death of John C. Calhoun.

1850. Death of President Taylor, one year and four months after his inauguration.

Fillmore, 1850-1853.

1850. Clay's "Omnibus Bill" passed.

1852. Henry Clay and Daniel Webster died.

Pierce, 1853-1857.

1853. The Gadsden Treaty—27,000 square miles of territory acquired from Mexico for $10,000,000, and the Mexican line established.

1854. Kansas-Nebraska Bill passed; a bill which organized the two territories, and gave the inhabitants of each the right to decide whether their territory should be admitted into the Union as free or slave. This bill abrogated the Missouri Compromise, which provided that after 1820 slavery should be prohibited in all other territory west of the Mississippi and north of the southern boundary of Missouri.

1857. The Kansas War, caused by a rivalry between the pro-slavery and anti-slavery parties.

Buchanan, 1857-1861.

1857. The Dred Scott Decision.

1858. Minnesota admitted into the Union.

1859. John Brown seized upon the United States Arsenal at Harper's Ferry, and proclaimed freedom to slaves in that section. He was captured and hanged as a traitor.

1860. Oregon admitted into the Union.

1860. South Carolina seceded from the Union.

1861. Kansas admitted into the Union.

1861. Southern Confederacy organized at Montgomery, Alabama, with Jefferson Davis as President and Alexander H. Stephens as Vice-President. South Carolina, Mississippi, Florida, Alabama, Georgia, Louisiana, Texas, Arkansas, Virginia, Tennessee, and North Carolina formed the Confederacy.

Lincoln, 1861-1865.

1861. War with the Confederate States declared. CAUSES: The slavery agitation and the secession of the Southern States were the principal causes. Battle of Bull Run or Manassas Junction.

1862. Capture of Fort Donelson; battles of Shiloh, Seven Pines, Seven Days, Second of Manassas, Antietam, Perryville, and Fredericksburg.

1863. Emancipation Proclamation; battles of

Chancellorsville, Gettysburg, Chickamauga, Missionary Ridge, and the surrender of Vicksburg. West Virginia admitted into the Union.

1864. Grant made Lieutenant-General; Battle of the Wilderness; Battle between the *Kearsarge* and the *Alabama;* Battle of Winchester; Nevada admitted into the Union; Sherman's March to the Sea; Lincoln reelected.

1865. Petersburg and Richmond captured; General Lee surrendered his army to General Grant at Appomattox Court-House, April 9; President Lincoln assassinated at Ford's Theatre in Washington, by John Wilkes Booth, April 14.

Johnson, 1865-1869.

1865. General Johnston surrendered to General Sherman, April 26.

1866. Atlantic cable successfully laid between Ireland and Newfoundland, by Cyrus W. Field.

1867. Nebraska admitted into the Union; Alaska purchased from Russia for $7,200,000; Tenure-of-Office Bill passed; President Johnson impeached.

Grant, 1869-1877.

1869. Pacific Railroad opened.

1870. The Fifteenth Amendment became a part of the Constitution.

1871. Chicago fire—3,000 acres devastated.

1872. Alabama claims settled.

1873. Modoc War; Financial panic.

1876. Centennial Exposition at Philadelphia; Colorado admitted into the Union; the Custer slaughter.

1877. Electoral Commission.

Hayes, 1877-1881.

1877. Railroad strike; Indian war.

1879. Resumption of specie payment.

1880. Treaties (two.) with China, respecting commerce and immigration.

Garfield, 1881.

1881. July 2—President Garfield was assasinated in the Baltimore and Potomac depot at Washington by Charles J. Guiteau, a disappointed office-seeker. The President died after ten weeks of great suffering.

Arthur, 1881-1885.

1881. Centennial anniversary of the capture of Yorktown.

1882. Execution of Charles J. Guiteau.

1883. The Civil Service Bill passed.

Cleveland, 1885-1889.

1885. Deaths of General U. S. Grant and Vice-President Hendricks.

1886. Presidential Succession Bill passed.

1887. Chicago anarchists hanged.

Harrison, 1889-1893.

1889. Oklahoma opened for settlement.

1889. The Conemaugh disaster, or the Johnstown flood.

1889. Admission of North Dakota, South Dakota, Montana, and Washington.

1890. Admission of Idaho and Wyoming.

1890. War with the Sioux Indians begins, and Sitting-Bull, the great Sioux chief, is killed.

1891. Deaths of General William T. Sherman, William Windom (Secretary of Treasury), George Bancroft, and James Russell Lowell.

1892. Dispute with Chili settled.

1892. Deaths of George William Curtis, John Greenleaf Whittier, Cyrus W. Field, and Jay Gould.

1892. Labor troubles at Homestead, Pennsylvania.
1892. Ex-President Grover Cleveland re-elected, after a vacation of one term.
1893. Deaths of Benjamin F. Butler and John E. Kenna.

Geography.

1. Geography is a description of the earth.
2. Physical Geography treats of the natural divisions of the earth's surface, [of the air, of the planets, and of the animals.
3. Mathematical Geography treats of the earth as a planet of the solar system, and how to represent the earth's surface on maps and globes.
4. Political Geography treats of the earth as divided by man, and of the nations on the earth, as to their governments and laws, their moral and social ndition, their language, their religion and national customs.
5. A Planet is a spherical body revolving around the sun, and receiving heat and light from it.
6. A Primary Planet is one which revolves around the sun as a center.
7. A Secondary Planet is one which revolves around a primary planet.
8. The Principal Planets named: (1.) In their order from the sun, Mercury, Venus, Earth, Mars, Jupiter, Saturn, Uranus, Neptune; (2.) In order of their sizes, Jupiter, Saturn, Neptune, Uranus, Earth, Venus, Mars, Mercury.

9. **The Orbit** of a planet is the path it describes around the sun. The earth's orbit is called the *Ecliptic*.

SHAPE OF THE EARTH.

10. **The Shape of the Earth** is that of a globe, ball, or sphere. The earth is not a perfect sphere; it is flattened at the poles, the polar diameter being twenty-six miles less than the equatorial diameter.

11. Proofs of the Earth's Sphericity.
 (1.) It has been circumnavigated.
 (2.) The appearance of approaching objects.
 (3.) The circular shape of the horizon.
 (4.) It casts a circular shadow on the moon during an eclipse of the moon.
 (5.) By actual measurement it has been found to be that of an *oblate spheroid*.
 (6.) All other planets are globular.

MOTIONS OF THE EARTH.

12. **The Earth has two Motions,**—one *diurnal* on its own axis, and one *annual* around the sun. *Day* and *night* proceed from the first motion, and the *four seasons* from the second.

The central line of the earth's rotation is called its *axis*. The ends of the axis are called *poles*.

The earth's axis is inclined $23\frac{1}{2}$ degrees from a perpendicular to the ecliptic.

CIRCLES OF THE EARTH.

13. Circles of the earth are imaginary lines passing around it. The earth is divided into two equal parts by *great circles*. All circles that divide the earth into two unequal parts are called *small circles*, as the parallels.

GEOGRAPHY.

14. The Equator is a great circle encompassing the globe from east to west, midway between the poles.

15. The Meridian Circles are great circles passing around the earth from north to south through the poles.

16. Meridians are semicircles of longitude, drawn from one pole to the other.

17. Parallels of Latitude are circles drawn around the earth parallel to the equator.

18. The Arctic Circle is a parallel $23\frac{1}{2}$ degrees from the North Pole.

19. The Antarctic Circle is a parallel $23\frac{1}{2}$ degrees from the South Pole.

20. The Tropics are parallels which mark the highest latitude which recives the vertical rays of the sun. They are located $23\frac{1}{2}$ degrees from the equator.

LATITUDE AND LONGITUDE.

21. Latitude is distance measured north and south of the equator.

22. Longitude is the distance east or west of an established meridian. It is measured 180 degrees east and west of the prime meridian.

ZONES.

23. Zones are belts or divisions of the earth's surface, parallel to the equator.

24. The Torrid Zone is 47 degrees wide, and lies between the northern and southern limits of the tropics.

25. The Temperate Zones lie, one *north* between the Tropic of Cancer and the Arctic Circle, and one *south* between the Tropic of Capricorn and the Antarctic Circle. They are each 43 degrees wide.

26. The Frigid Zones lie, one *north* between the North Pole and the Arctic Circle, and one *south* be-

tween the South Pole and the Antarctic Circle. They are each 23½ degrees wide.

GENERAL DEFINITIONS.

27. **The Horizon** is the point where the earth and sky seem to meet.

28. **The Horizon Circle** is the line which bounds our view on the earth's surface.

29. **The Zenith** is the point directly overhead.

30. **The Nadir** is the point directly under the place where we stand.

31. **Antipodes** are persons who live on the opposite side of the earth from us.

32. **Equinoctial Points** are points where the sun crosses the equator. The word *Equinox* means equal nights. The *vernal equinox* occurs the 20th of March; the *autumnal equinox* on the 22d of September.

33. **The Solstitial Points** are the northern and southern limits of the sun. The *summer solstice* occurs on the 21st of June, and the *winter solstice* on the 21st of December.

34. **Islands** are bodies of land smaller than continents, entirely surrounded by water.

35. **Continental Islands** are those lying near the shores of the continents.

36. **Oceanic Islands** are those lying far from the shores of the continents.

37. **Volcanic Islands** are those which have been formed by volcanoes.

38. **Coral Islands** are those which have been formed by coral animals.

39. **A Peninsula** (*pene*, almost, *insula*, an island) is a portion of land almost surrounded by water.

40. An Isthmus is a narrow neck of land uniting two larger portions of land.
41. A Cape is a point of land jutting out into the sea.
42. A Plain is a great extent of land slightly raised above the ocean.
43. A Plateau is a plain one thousand feet or more above the level of the sea.
44. A Prairie is a large, treeless plain, found in the United States.
45. A Pampas is a large, treeless plain, found in the south-eastern part of South America, in the valley of the La Plata.
46. The Llanos are plains of the Orinoco River. They are covered with verdure in the rainy season, and in the dry season they are barren.
47. Silvas are extensive plains in the valley of the Amazon River.
48. A Desert is a barren tract of land, usually covered with sand.
49. An Oasis is a fertile spot in a desert.
50. An Ocean is the largest natural division of water.
51. A Sea is a large body of water smaller than an ocean.
52. A Lake is a body of water surrounded by land.
53. A Gulf or Bay is a portion of water extending into the land.
54. A Strait is a narrow passage of water joining two larger portions of water.
55. A Bank is a shallow part of the sea.
56. The Oceanic Movements are waves, tides, and currents.
57. Waves are the rise and fall of the ocean waters, caused by the wind.

58. **Tides** are the periodical risings and fallings of the waters of the ocean, caused by the unequal attractions of the sun and the moon.

59. **Ocean Currents** are vast streams of water flowing through the ocean. They are produced by the combined action of the *heat of the sun*, the *rotation of the earth*, and the *tides* and *winds*.

60. **The Great Equatorial Current** is the most important of the ocean currents. It is a broad stream of warm water, and flows constantly on both sides of the equator.

61. **The Atlantic Equatorial Current** flows from the western coast of Africa towards America. It divides into two branches, one flowing south along the coast of Brazil, and the other flowing north-west into the Caribbean Sea, and thence, passing around the Gulf of Mexico, it is finally driven through the Florida Strait, where it receives the name of the *Gulf Stream*.

62. **The Gulf Stream** flows north-east from Florida Strait to Newfoundland, where it turns and divides into two branches. One of these branches flows towards Great Britain, and thence to Norway; the other, passing around the Azores, unites with the Equatorial Current.

63. **The Pacific Equatorial Current** flows west from South America to Asia. It divides into two branches. One of these branches flows along the coast of New Guinea and Australia, and passes into the Antarctic Current; the other branch flows north-east along the coast of Asia to the Aleutian Islands, and thence passes down the coast of America to California. This is called the *Japan Current*.

GEOGRAPHY. 33

64. **A River** is a large stream of water flowing in a channel to the sea, a lake, or another river.

65. **A River System** consists of a number of rivers emptying into the same body of water.

66. **A River Basin** is the entire area drained by a river and its branches.

67. **A Delta** is the land enclosed between the mouths of a river. They are formed by the deposit of mud and sediment carried down by the river.

68. **A Firth, or Estuary,** is the open or wide mouth of a river.

69. **A Spring** is water issuing spontaneously from the earth.

70. **Thermal Springs** discharge hot water, and are caused by the streams of water in the earth coming in contact with heated portions of the earth's crust, which converts part of the water into steam, thus causing the water to pass through its channels with such force that vast columns of water are sometimes thrown many feet above the surface of the earth.

71. **Geysers** are thermal springs, the waters of which are sometimes thrown hundreds of feet above the surface of the earth.

72. **Artesian Wells** are artificial springs made by boring through the crust of the earth, until a reservoir of water is reached whose source is higher than the surface at the point of boring. The water flows through the opening to the surface of the earth, and is often thrown in a continuous jet with great force.

73. **The Atmosphere** is the elastic gaseous substance which surrounds the earth to the height of about fifty miles.

74. **Wind** is air in motion. It is caused by the

unequal heating of the atmosphere. Winds are classified as *Permanent*, *Variable*, and *Periodical*.

75. **Trade Winds** are formed within the tropics, and blow in a westerly direction throughout the year. They received their name from the assistance they rendered to trade, before the invention of steamers.

76. **Climate** is the condition of the atmosphere as to temperature, winds, moisture, and salubrity.

77. **Dew** is the moisture which gathers upon vegetation and other bodies during the clear summer nights.

78. **Clouds** are formed from the condensed vapors rising from the earth, and differ from fog only in occupying higher regions of the atmosphere.

79. **Rain.**—When the watery vapor in the clouds is condensed, it falls to the earth in the form of *rain*.

80. **Snow** is vapor suddenly condensed into a semi-solid state by freezing.

81. **Hail** is formed out of rain-drops that freeze as they fall through colder regions of the atmosphere. Several theories have been advanced respecting the formation of hailstones. The rotary theory is, that a snow-flake being formed is carried, as in a cyclone, down into the moist, warm air, where it receives a layer of moisture, and then back into the cold, when it is frozen. This process alternates in cold and warm air, until layer after layer being added, the stone thus formed becomes too heavy to be carried by the rotating wind, and falls to the earth.

Physiology.

1. **The Three Kingdoms of Nature** are the *mineral*, the *vegetable*, and the *animal*.

2. **Organic Bodies** are those having organs by which they grow; as, *plants* and *animals*.

3. **Inorganic Bodies** are those which are naturally destitute of life; as, *air, water, minerals*.

4. **An Organ** is a portion of an organized body, having some special function, or duty.

5. **Anatomy** treats of the structure, form, number, and position of the organs of the body.

6. **Physiology** treats of the functions, or duties, of the different organs.

7. **Hygiene** is that department of knowledge which treats of the preservation of health.

8. **A System** is several organs similar in structure taken together.

9. **The Bones** are the frame work of the body, and serve (1.) to preserve the shape of the body; (2.) to protect some important organs; and (3.) to furnish a firm surface for the attachment of the muscles.

10. **The Bones are Composed** of animal matters and mineral matters.

11. **Ossification** is the process by which animal matter (jelly) is changed into bone by the deposition of calcareous matter.

12. **The Periosteum** is a fibrous membrane covering the exterior surface of the bones, except at the joints.

13. The **Membranes** of the body are divided into the *mucous* and the *serous* membranes.

14. Mucous Membranes line all the cavities and passages of the body which have external communication, and are continuous with the skin, and with each other.

15. Serous Membranes line all the cavities of the body which are without any external communication.

16. Muscles are animal tissues, usually known as *lean meat*. There are more than five hundred muscles in the human body.

17. A Tendon is a hard and strong cord by which a muscle is attached to a bone.

18. The Skin is the natural covering of the body, and is the organ of touch. It is composed of two layers,—the *epidermis* and *dermis*.

19. A Gland is an organ which secretes and pours forth a liquid which passes out through tubes.

20. The Glands of the Skin are of two kinds,—the *sweat glands*, and the *sebaceous*, or *oil glands*.

21. A Sweat Gland consists of a tube, which is coiled into a ball, ascending to the surface of the skin. The secretion is called *sweat*, or *perspiration*.

22. The Sebaceous Glands (oil glands) are found in the dermis, usually about the roots of the hair, being most abundant in the scalp and face. They secrete an oily substance, which annoints the hair and keeps the skin soft and moist.

23. Digestion is the process by which food in the alimentary canal is so changed that it can be absorbed by the lymphatics and the blood-vessels.

24. The Organs of Digestion are the *mouth, tongue,*

teeth, salivary glands, pharynx, œsophagus, stomach, intestines, lacteals, thoracic duct, liver, and *pancreas.*

25. **The Teeth** in man are of two sets,—the *temporary* (twenty in number) and the *permanent* (thirty-two in number). Most all animals are provided with two sets of teeth.

26. **The Salivary Glands** consist of three glands on each side of the mouth. They secrete a liquid called *saliva.*

27. **The Pharynx,** or *throat,* is a muscular, membraneous sac, about four inches long, leading to the œsophagus.

28. **The Œsophagus,** or *gullet,* is a muscular tube, about nine inches long, extending from the pharynx to the stomach.

29. **The Stomach** is a large pouch, situated in the left side of the abdomen, and extending from the œsophagus to the small intestine. It will hold from one to two quarts; but it may be distended so as to hold as much as three quarts.

30. **The Intestines** are a tube about thirty feet in length, filling a greater part of the abdomen. They are divided into the *small intestine* and the *large intestine.*

31. **The Lacteals** are small tubes, or vessels, for conveying chyle from the intestines to the thoracic duct.

32. **The Thoracic Duct** commences just below the diaphragm, and ascends in front of the spinal column to the apex of the chest, where it turns downward and forward, and ends in the left sub clavian vein. It is about the diameter of a goose-quill.

33. **The Liver** is the largest and busiest gland of

the body. It is of a reddish brown color, tinged with yellow. Its principal function is to secrete bile.

34. **The Pancreas** is a gland about six inches long, situated behind the stomach. It secretes pancreatic juice.

35. **The Processes of Digestion** are (1.) mastication and insalivation, (2.) deglutition (swallowing), (3.) chymification, (4.) chylification, and (5.) absorption. 1. The food is taken into the mouth, where it is ground fine by the teeth and mixed with the saliva—(*mastication and insalivation*). 2. It then passes from the mouth through the pharynx and the œsophagus into the stomach—(*deglutition*). 3. In the stomach it is thoroughly mixed with the gastric juice, which converts it into a pulpy substance of a dark color, called chyme—(*chymification*). 4. It then passes through the pyloric orifice into the small intestine, where it is subjected to the intestinal juice, the bile, and the pancreatic fluid, which finish the dissolution of all nutritive food, and change it into a milky-like fluid called chyle—(*chylification*). 5. The chyle is absorbed from the small intestine by the lacteals and the blood-vessels, and the lacteals pour their contents into the thoracic duct, which leads to the sub-clavian vein—(*absorption*).

36. **Circulation** is the regular flow of the blood through the different blood-vessels of the body.

37. **The Blood** is the circulating fluid of the body. It is made up of a transparent fluid called *plasma*, and minute circular bodies called *corpuscles*, which float in the plasma. The corpuscles are of two kinds,—the *red* and the *white*.

38 **The Organs of Circulation** are the *heart, arteries, veins,* and *capillaries.*

39. The Heart is a hollow muscular organ, situated between the lungs in the thorax. In the adult man it is about the size of the closed fist. It is divided by a muscular partition into two chambers, the *right* and the *left* heart. Each chamber is divided into two cavities, the *auricle* and the *ventricle*.

40. The Arteries are tough cylindrical tubes which convey the blood from the heart to different parts of the body.

41. The Veins are cylindrical tubes which carry the blood from the different parts of the body to the heart.

42. The Capillaries are minute blood-vessels which connect the termination of the arteries with the commencement of the veins.

43. The Course of the Circulation: The dark, impure blood is forced from the right ventricle into the pulmonary artery, and thence to the capillaries of the lungs. After being purified in the lungs, it is conveyed through the pulmonary veins to the left auricle, then through the mitral valves into the left ventricle. This is called the *pulmonary circulation.*

By a contraction of the left ventricle the blood passes through the aortic semilunar valves into the aorta; and through its branches the blood is conveyed to all parts of the body, from which it returns through the capillaries and veins to the right auricle. This is called the *systemic circulation.*

44. The Organs of Respiration are (1.) the *air-passages*, through which the air enters and leaves the lungs; (2.) the *lungs*, in which the blood is exposed to the action of the air; and (3.) certain muscles used in breathing.

45. **The Air Passages** include the *nostril chambers*, the *pharynx* (throat), the *larynx*, the *trachea*, the *bronchia*, and the *air-cells*.

46. **The Lungs** are two in number, and lie inside the thorax (chest), one on each side of the heart. They are elastic, spongy masses, full of tiny cavities, called *air-cells*.

47. **The Diaphragm** is a thin, broad, circular partition, separating the abdomen from the chest.

48. **Respiration** is the breathing of air into (inspiration) and out of (expiration) the lungs.

49. **The Nervous System** is composed of the *brain*, the *spinal cord*, the *ganglionic system*, and the *nerves*.

50. **The Brain** is the great center of the nervous system, and it is the seat of the mind. It is a pulpy mass found in the cavity of the skull, and is made up of two parts,—the *cerebrum*, which occupies the upper and anterior parts of the cranium, and the *cerebellum*, the lower and smaller portion.

51. **The Spinal Cord** is the cylindrical long mass of nerve-matter found in the spinal canal. It extends from the pons to the second lumbar vertebra.

52. **The Pons** is the bridge of nerve fibres connecting the cerebrum, the cerebellum, and the spinal cord.

53. **The Medulla Oblongata** is the upper enlarged part of the spinal cord. It is about one inch long, and lies within the skull.

54. **The Sympathetic System** (Ganglionic) consists of two nerves, one on each side, containing many ganglia. They extend the whole length of the spinal column.

55. **Nerves** are small white cords of nervous matter, used to conduct the nervous influence.

56. **The Organs of Special Sense** are the *tongue*, the *nose*, the *ear*, the *eye*, and the *skin*.

Civil Government.

1. Government is the organized power by which a State or nation is ruled.
2. Civil Government is the power which regulates the rights and duties of the citizens of a country.

3. General Forms of Government.
(1.) Monarchy, or government by one person.
(2.) Aristocracy, or government by a few select persons.
(3.) Democracy, or government by the people.

4. Kinds of Monarchies.
(1.) Absolute Monarchy, where the power is unlimited.
(2.) Limited Monarchy, where the power is limited by law.

5. Kinds of Democracies.
(1.) Pure or Absolute Democracy, where all the voters meet together to make and execute their laws.
(2.) Representative Democracy, or *Republic*, where the voters choose representatives to make and execute their laws.

6. Departments of Government.
(1.) Legislative, or law-making.
(2.) Executive, or law-enforcing.
(3.) Judicial, or law-interpreting.

7. Kinds of Colonial Government.

(1.) **Provincial or Royal Government,** or that under the direct control of the king, as in New York and the Carolinas.

(2.) **Proprietary Government,** or that in which certain person, called proprietors, exercised the power, as in Pennsylvania, Delaware, and Maryland.

(3.) **Charter Government,** or that in which limited powers and rights were vested in the colonists, by a charter from the king, as in Massachusetts, Rhode Island, and Connecticut.

8. **A Charter** is a grant made by a sovereign to a people, securing to them the enjoyment of certain rights; or it is the fundamental law of a country. It differs from a constitution in being granted by a sovereign, and not established by the people.

9. **A Constitution** is the fundamental law of a country, setting forth the principles upon which the government is founded, the rights of the citizens, and the manner in which the governmental powers are organized, distributed, and administered.

10. **A Preamble** is the introductory part of a constitution or a statute, and contains a declaration of the designs or motives of the framers.

11. Periods of the United States Government.

(1.) **The Revolutionary,** extending from the time of the meeting of the first Continental Congress, September 5, 1774, to the final ratification of the Articles of Confederation, March 1, 1781.

(2.) **The Confederate,** extending from 1781 to 1789, when the present Constitution went into operation.

(3.) **The Constitutional,** extending from 1789 to the present time.

CIVIL GOVERNMENT. 43

12. **The Declaration of Independence** was a document in which the Thirteen English Colonies of America declared themselves free and independent. By its adoption by the Continental Congress, July 4, 1776, these colonies became the Thirteen United States of America.

13. **The Articles of Confederation** was the constitution or body of laws by which the United States were governed from 1781 to 1789. They were adopted by Congress in 1777, but they did not go into effect until 1781.

14. **The Constitutional Convention** met at Philadelphia (1787) to revise the Articles of Confederation, but it was found that they contained too many defects for a successful revision. They gave not enough power to Congress to make it a strong central government, and left the States almost sovereign and independent. Congress could not collect a dollar, enlist a single soldier, nor regulate commerce. It could suggest, but it could not compel. The convention abandoned the original purpose, and prepared an entirely new constitution, the Federal Constitution, which was adopted in 1787.

15. Purposes of the Federal Constitution.
(1.) To form a more perfect union.
(2.) To establish justice.
(3.) To insure domestic tranquillity.
(4.) To provide for the common defense.
(5.) To promote the general welfare.
(6.) To secure the blessings of liberty to the people.

16. **The Legislative Department**—all legislative powers vested in a Congress of the United States, which consists of a Senate and House of Representatives.

17. Representatives.

(1.) Chosen by the people every second year.

(2.) Necessary qualifications—not less than twenty-five years of age, seven years a citizen, and must be an inhabitant of the State in which he shall be chosen.

(3.) Apportioned according to population.

(4.) Vacancies—filled by a special election.

18. Senators.

(1.) Number—two from each State.

(2.) Term of office—six years.

(3.) Elected by the State Legislatures of the respective States.

(4.) Necessary qualifications—must have attained to the age of thirty years, must have been nine years a citizen of the United States, and must be an inhabitant of the State for which he is chosen.

(5.) *Vacancies* in the Senate are filled by an appointment made by the governor, if the Legislature is not in session.

19. **The Vice-President** of the United States is President of the Senate.

20. **An Impeachment** is a written accusation charging a civil officer of the United States with treason, bribery, or other high crime or misdemeanor.

REMARK.—The House of Representatives has the sole power to prepare articles of impeachment, but the Senate has the sole power to try all impeachments. When the President of the United States is tried, the Chief-justice presides. A two-thirds vote is necessary to convict. Judgment extends no farther than to removal from office, and disqualification to hold and enjoy any office of honor, trust, or profit under the United States; but the offender may afterwards be brought to trial and punishment in a court of law, the same as any private citizen.

21. **Revenue Bills** are bills by which money is raised for the government. They must originate in the House of Representatives.

22. **Customs**, or *Duties*, are taxes levied upon certain articles imported from foreign countries. The taxation of exports is prohibited by the Constitution.

23. **A Tariff** is a schedule of dutiable goods, with the rate upon each article.

24. **A Direct Tax** is one levied directly at a given rate on property or polls.

25. **An Indirect Tax** is one levied on articles of consumption.

26. **An Excise** (*internal revenue*) is a tax on articles manufactured and used within the country, and also on various kinds of business.

27. **Naturalization** is the legal process by which an alien or foreigner may become a citizen of the United States.

PROCESS: He must appear in court, declare his intention to become a citizen, and his purpose to renounce all allegiance to foreign governments; and after two years he must re-appear in open court, and make oath or affirm that he renounces all foreign allegiance, and will support the Constitution of the United States. He must have resided in the United States for, at least, five years next preceding the date of his final appearance in court.

28. **The High Seas** include the waters of the ocean which are out of sight of land, also the waters of the sea-coast below low-water mark, whether within the boundaries of a nation or state.

29. **Letters of Marque and Reprisal** are commissions from the government, authorizing private individuals to seize the property of a foreign state, or of its citizens or subjects, as a satisfaction for an injury committed.

30. **A Writ of Habeas Corpus** is a writ issued by a court, directed to a person charged with detaining another unlawfully in his custody, commanding him to bring the body of the prisoner into court, and to show cause of his detention.

31. **A Bill of Attainder** is an act of a legislative body, inflicting the penalty of death upon a person accused of crime, without a regular trial before a court.

32. **An Ex-post-facto Law** is one passed after the act to which it refers has been committed, making the act criminal, which was not so when committed.

33. **Executive Department**—vested in a President of the United States.

34. **The Electoral College** consists of the whole body of *electors* chosen by the people of the respective states, to vote for President and Vice-President.

35. The President.

(1.) Commander-in-chief of the United States army and navy.

(2.) Term of office—four years.

(3.) Elected by the Electoral College (since 1887, second Monday in January).

(4.) His necessary qualifications—natural born citizen, at least thirty-five years of age, and fourteen years a resident of the United States.

(5.) The Vice-President succeeds him, in case of a vacancy.

(6.) The Presidential Succession Law of 1886 provides that the members of the Cabinet succeed each other in the following order: Secretary of State, Secretary of Treasury, Secretary of War, Attorney-General, Postmaster-General, Secretary of Navy, Secretary of Interior, and Secretary of Agriculture.

36. **Judicial Department** is vested in one Supreme Court (established by the Constitution) and two regular inferior courts, the Circuit and District Courts, and a number of other courts for certain purposes, established by Congress.

REMARK.—The Supreme Court consists of one Chief-Justice and eight associate judges. The United States is divided into nine judicial circuits, and the nine judges of the Supreme Court are each assigned to one of these divisions; and for each circuit there is also appointed a circuit judge. The lowest regular court in the federal system is the District Court. There is at least one district for each state, but some states are divided into two districts, and have a judge for each. New York and Texas are each divided into three judicial districts. The entire Union contains about sixty of these districts.

37. Federal Judges.

(1.) How chosen—nominated by the President and confirmed by the Senate.

(2.) Term of office—during good behavior, but may retire on salary, at the age of seventy years, after having served ten years.

(3.) Salaries—Chief-Justice, $10,500 per year; Associate Justices, $10,000; Circuit Judges, $6,000; District Judges, from $3,500 to $5,000.

Book-Keeping.

1. **Book-keeping** is the science of accounts, and the art of recording business transactions.
2. **Single Entry Book-keeping** is that system in which only one entry, a debit or a credit, is usually made in the Ledger for a single business transaction, accounts being kept usually with persons only.
3. **Double Entry Book-keeping** is that system in which at least two entries, a debit and a credit, are made for a single business transaction, accounts being kept with persons, and also with everything that affects the financial workings and condition of the business.
4. **An Account** is a statement of business transactions.
5. **Resources**, or *Assets*, are available means, and comprise all kinds of property or anything from which value may be realized, such as Cash, Merchandise, Real Estate, Notes, and Debts due from others.
6. **Liabilities** are obligations to pay, and comprise all personal Debts, Notes, or other obligations requiring payment to others.
7. **Capital** is money or property used for carrying on a business.
8. **Net Capital** is the excess of resources over liabilities.
9. **Net Insolvency** is the excess of liabilities over resources.
10. **Net Gain** is the excess of net capital at closing over net capital at beginning.

11. **Net Loss** is the excess of net capital at beginning over net capital at closing.

12. **A Transaction** is the act of buying or selling.

13. **A Debtor** is one who owes another.

14. **A Creditor** is one who is owed by another.

15. **Debit** means to charge with debt. The term is also applied to that side of an account which shows what is owed, or the debtor side.

16. **Books used in Single Entry.**—The Day Book and the Ledger are the principal books used in Single Entry; but where the business is extensive, the Cash Book, Bill Book, Invoice Book, Sales Book, etc., are also generally used. These are termed *auxiliary books*.

17. **The Day Book** is a book of original entry in which transactions requiring a debit or a credit are recorded in the order of their occurrence.

18. **The Ledger** is the final book of entry, or the book in which all sums entered in books of original entry are arranged under appropriate titles, or under their proper heads.

19. **The Cash Book** is the book in which all receipts and payments of cash are entered.

20. **The Bill Book** is the book used for recording all promissory notes, and other written obligations, received or issued.

21. **The Invoice Book** is the book used for preserving invoices of goods bought.

22. **The Sales Book** is the book in which a record of all sales is kept.

23. **The Journal** is a book used in Double Entry for recording transactions first written in the Day Book, the Sales Book, or the Invoice Book. It is the intermediate book between these books and the Ledger.

Its office is to decide upon the proper debits and credits involved in each transaction, preparatory to their going upon the Ledger.

24. **The Journal Day Book.**—The essential facts commonly recorded in the Day Book may be written in the Journal, so as to make the Journal serve the double purpose of the two books. The book thus used is called by some authors the *Journal Day Book;* but in business it is called either the *Day Book* or the *Journal.*

25. **Posting** is the process of transferring accounts from the Journal, or from books of original entry, to the Ledger.

26. **Books of Original Entry** are those which contain statements in detail of business transactions. The Day Book is the principal book of original entry.

27. **Opening Books** is making such entries as are necessary to show the condition of affairs at the time of beginning business.

28. **Closing Books** is making such entries as are necessary to show the condition of the business, or the financial condition of an individual or a firm.

29. **The Classes of Accounts** are (1.) Personal Accounts, or those kept with persons, firms, or corporations; (2.) Real Accounts, or accounts kept with property of any kind, as, Cash, Merchandise, Real Estate, Bills Receivable, Bills Payable, etc.; (3.) Imaginary Accounts, or accounts to which fictitious titles are applied to represent the person or persons conducting the business, or to supply the want of a real name. Stock, Expense, and Interest accounts belong to this class of accounts.

30. **Titles of Accounts** are the names by which ac-

counts are known. In Single Entry, accounts are usually kept with persons only. Sometimes a Cash account, a Merchandise account, a Bills Receivable account, a Bills Payable account, or an Expense account is kept in a Single Entry Leger; but when such is the case it ceases to be purely Single Entry, and approaches Double Entry, although it lacks many of the valuable features of Double Entry.

31. **Personal Accounts** are accounts kept with persons or firms. The name of each person or firm is the title of the account.

32. **Stock** is a title employed to represent the person or firm conducting the business.

33. **Merchandise** embraces all the usual articles of trade; as, Dry Goods, Groceries, Hardware, Wheat, Flour, etc. A separate account may be kept with any kind of merchandise, by giving the class its proper title.

34. **Cash** includes all cash items; as, Specie, Bank Bills, Bank Checks, Sight Drafts, etc.

35. **Bills Receivable** include all written promises of others, payable at a future time, which come into our possession, and on which we are entitled to *receive* payment; as, Notes, Drafts, Acceptances, etc.

36. **Bills Payable** include all our written promises issued to others, payable at a future time.

37. **Expense** is the title of the account under which we enter all amounts expended for carrying on the business; as, Rent, Freight, Salaries, Fuel, etc.

38. **Profit and Loss** is the title of the account which shows the profits and losses in business. The debit side contains the *losses*, the credit side the *gains;* and the difference shows the *net gain* or the *net loss.*

39. General Rules for Journalizing.

Rule 1. The PROPRIETOR is *credited* for the sum of his resources at the beginning of business, for all subsequent investments, and for his net gain in the business.

Rule 2. The PROPRIETOR is *debited* for the sum of his liabilities at the beginning of business, for what he draws from the business, and for his net loss in the business.

Rule 3. PERSONS are *debited* when they become indebted to us, or when we get out of their debt.

Rule 4. PERSONS are *credited* when we become indebted to them, or when they get out of our debt.

Rule 5. PROPERTY (Cash, Merchandise, Bills Payable, Bills Receivable, etc.) is *debited* when we receive it, and *credited* when we part with it.

Teaching.

1. **Education** is the process of securing rational freedom through the subordination of the powers of the mind and the organs of the body, to the laws of reason and morality.

2. **The Kinds of Education.**—The process of education is generally divided into *Physical*, *Intellectual*, and *Moral* education.

3. **Physical Education** is that which pertains to the body, and has for its object the proper training of every power of the body for the attainment of health, strength, skill, grace, and beauty.

4. **Intellectual Education** is that which pertains to the intellect, and has for its object the training, growth, and development of the intellectual powers of man.

5. **Moral Education** is that which pertains to the moral nature of man. Its object is the cultivation of the conscience and the subordination of the will to one's sense of right and duty.

6. **The Mind** is that which thinks, feels, and wills. The terms *mind* and *soul* are used by some authors as synonymous; others apply the term *mind* to the intellect or knowing power of the soul.

7. **Consciousness** is the mind knowing itself and its own activities and states.

8. **A Mental Faculty** is the capability of the mind to put forth a distinct form of activity. It is the mind's power to act in a definite way. The mind possesses as many faculties as there are distinct forms of mental activity.

9. **The Mind or Soul** embraces three general classes of faculties,—the *Intellect*, the *Sensibilities*, and the *Will*.

10. **The Intellect** is the mind's power to think and to know. Its products are *ideas* and *thoughts*. It includes a number of faculties,—*perception, memory, imagination, understanding,* and *intuition,* or the *reason*.

11. **The Sensibilities** are the powers by which we feel. Their products are *emotions, affections, desires,* and *appetites*.

12. **The Will** is the mental activity of choosing and determining. It is the executive power of the mind.

13. **Perception** is the power of the mind to know immediately and directly external objects; or it is the

faculty by which a knowledge of the qualities of objects is gained through the senses.

14. **Memory** is the power of the mind to retain and recall knowledge, or previous acquisitions.

15. **Imagination** is the power by which the mind holds up before itself the images which are called up by recollection; or it is the power of the mind by which objects previously known are represented and modified, or recombined.

16. **Understanding** is the power by which the relations of things to each other are determined; or it is the power by which we compare objects of thought and derive abstract and general ideas and truths. It embraces *Abstraction, Conception, Judgment,* and *Reasoning.*

17. **Intuition, or the Reason,** is that power of the mind which makes us acquainted with simple primary ideas and truths; or it is that power by which we know certain ideas and truths without being taught.

18. **Abstraction** is the process by which the mind draws a quality away from its object and makes it an object of special consideration.

19. **Conception** is the power of forming general notions. It unites a number of qualities common to many individuals, and produces a single complex mental representative of all these individuals taken as a class.

20. **Judgment** is the power of comparing objects of thought or observation, and deciding as to their agreements or disagreements, their resemblances or differences, etc.

21. **Reasoning** is the process of comparing two ideas through their relation to a third.

22. **Inductive Reasoning** is the process of deriving a general truth from particular truths. Thus, if we observe that all perfect apples examined by us have five seeds, we may infer that all perfect apples everywhere will have the same number.

23. **Deductive Reasoning** is the process of deriving a particular truth from a general truth. Thus, from the general proposition that all perfect apples have five seeds, we may infer by *deduction* that any particular perfect apple will have five seeds.

24. **Attention** is the concentration of mental energy and activity upon any one object of thought.

Methods of Cultivating Each Faculty.

25. **Perception.**—The Perceptive Powers are most active in early childhood, and should be carefully cultivated during this period of life. Since the child obtains a knowledge of the outside world through the five senses, this act of the mind in knowing is often called sense-perception. It may be properly called the perceptive activity, or the activity of perceiving. Nature gives active senses to a little child, therefore the perceptive powers are cultivated by training children to a habit of close observation. Children should be required to describe objects, and draw their outlines. Since observation is the source of all knowledge, it is important that children be taught the habit of using their perceptive powers.

26. **The Memory.**—To cultivate the Memory, (1.) Require the pupils to give close attention to the subject they are considering; (2.) Lead them to feel an interest in the subject; (3.) Require them to review that which they have previously studied; (4.) Require them to memorize extracts of prose and poetry; (5.)

Teach them to connect their knowledge by the laws of association.

27. **The Imagination.**—The Imagination may be cultivated by observing the beautiful in the scenes of nature and art, and by reading poetry, fiction, books of travel, and other imaginative compositions.

28. **Attention.**—The power of Attention may be cultivated, (1.) By requiring the pupils to observe objects closely; (2.) By requiring them to study with close attention; (3.) By requiring them to repeat problems in mental arthmetic, and give their solutions, without the use of a book; (4.) By requiring them to write long sentences from memory.

29. **Educational Laws.**—The following are the most important of the general laws of education:

1. The human mind embraces a number of distinct faculties.
2. The faculties of the mind develop in a fixed orde .
3. Self activity is a law of mental growth.
4. The mind is both acquisitive and productive.
5. Human beings are created with different tastes and talents.
6. The human mind is finite.

30. **Principles of Instruction.**—The following principles indicate the laws by which the teacher should be governed in imparting instruction so that the mind of the child may be properly trained and developed:

1. The primary object of teaching is to afford culture.
2. Exercise is necessary to culture.
3. The perceptive powers should receive early and careful culture.

4. The order of instruction should correspond to the order of growth.

5. All primary instruction should proceed from the known to the most nearly related unknown.

6. All primary instruction should be given in the concrete.

7. Instruction should first be inductive, then deductive.

8. Ideas should first be taught, then words.

Grammar.

A Synopsis of the Parts of Speech.

The Noun.

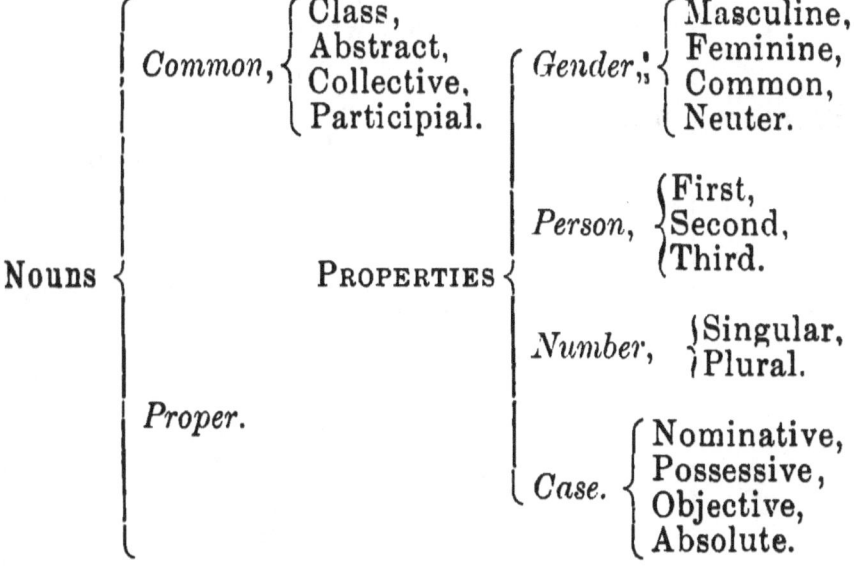

GRAMMAR.

The Adjective.

- Adjectives
  - *Descriptive,*
    - Common,
    - Proper,
    - Participial.
  - *Definitive.*
    - Article,
      - Definite,
      - Indefinite.
    - Pronominal,
      - Demonstrative,
      - Distributive,
      - Indefinite.
    - Numeral.
      - Cardinal,
      - Ordinal,
      - Multiplicative.

The Pronoun.

- Pronouns
  - *Personal,*
    - Simple,
      - I,
      - thou,
      - he, she, it.
    - Comp'd.
      - Myself,
      - thyself,
      - herself, himself, itself.
  - *Relative,*
    - Simple,
      - Who,
      - which,
      - what,
      - that,
      - as.
    - Comp'd.
      - Whoever, whoso, whosoever,
      - whichever, whichsoever,
      - whatever, whatsoever.
  - *Interrogative.*
    - Who,
    - which,
    - what.
  - PROPERTIES
    - Gender,
    - Person,
    - Number,
    - Case.

GRAMMAR. 59

The Verb.

Verbs
- *As to use:* Copulative, Transitive, Intransitive.
- *As to form:* Regular, Irregular.
- PROPERTIES
  - Voice: Active, Passive.
  - Mode: Indicative, Subjunctive, Potential, Imperative, Infinitive.
  - Tense:
    - Absolute: Present, Past, Future.
    - Relative: Pr. Perfect, Past ", Future ".
  - Number,
  - Person.
- *Sub-classes:* Defective, Redundant, Auxiliary.
- Participles: Present, Perfect, Compound.

The Adverb.

Adverbs
- Of Time,
- Of Place,
- Of Cause,
- Of Manner,
- Of Degree.

ALSO:
- Modal,
- Interrogative,
- Conjunctive.

The Conjunction.

Conjunctions
- *Co-ordinate,*
  - Copulative,
  - Adversative,
  - Alternative,
  - Illative.
- *Subordinate.*
  - Causal,
  - Temporal,
  - Local,
  - Of manner or degree.

A Synopsis of the English Sentence.

Sentences
- *As to use,*
  - Declarative,
  - Interrogative,
  - Imperative,
  - Exclamatory.
- *As to form,*
  - Simple,
  - Complex,
  - Compound.

Elements.

Elements
- *As to form,*
  - Simple,
  - Complex,
  - Compound.
- *As to composition,*
  - Words,
  - Phrases,
  - Clauses.
- *As to rank,*
  - Principal,
    - Subject,
    - Predicate.
  - Subordinate.
    - Objective,
    - Adjective,
    - Adverbial,
    - Connective.
    - Attendant.

A KEY

TO DIFFICULT CONSTRUCTIONS IN HARVEY'S ENGLISH GRAMMAR.

NOTE.—The first number indicates the page; the second, the number of the sentence, the comment following the numbers.

The author's aim is not to give the parsing and the analysis in full, but to discuss very briefly only the most difficult points.

42-1. *Doctor* is in apposition with the first *Johnson*, and *lawyer*, with the second.

42-2. *Queen Elizabeth* is in the possessive case, and modifies *reign*. *Reign* is the object of the preposition *in*.

42-6. *Quadrupeds, fowls, fishes, reptiles,* and *insects,* are in the objective case, in apposition with *classes*. *Classes* is neuter gender; *quadrupeds, fowls,* etc., are common gender.

42-7. *Army* is neuter, singular.

42-8. *Platos* and *Aristotles* are proper nouns, used as common nouns, and are nominative to *are*.

42-9. *Mr. Squires* is in the objective case, object of *have seen; bookseller* and *stationer* are in apposition with *Mr. Squires*.

53-3. *But a* may be parsed as a single adjective, modifying *vapor*. Some authors parse *but* as an adverb, modifying *is*.

53-5. *Sad* and *lonely* are predicate adjectives after *feel*, and limit *I*.

53-6. *Look* is the copula, and *green* is a predicate adjective, limiting the subject *fields*.

53-11. *Such a* limits the subject *law.* *Disgrace* is a noun, and is used as the predicate of the sentence.

53-13. *Powers* is in the absolute case. *Ye* is the subject of the sentence.

53-17. *None* is an adjective used as the subject of the sentence. *But great* equals *except great,* and modifies *none.* *Unhappy* belongs to *great.*

53-18. *But a* is an adjective; or *but* may be parsed as an adverb, modifying *is.*

53-19. *To make a long story short* is a complex attendant element. *Short* belongs to *story.* *Broke up* is a complex verb; or *up* may be parsed as an adverb.

54-21. *Have been lashed* is modified by *round and round circle,* by *for years,* and by (during) *session.*

54-22. *Shade* is the subject, *flits* is the copula, and *gray* is a predicate adjective, and belongs to *shade.* *Dim* belongs to *shade.*

54-23. *Back* is an adverb, modifying *can call.* *To mansion* modifies *can call.*

54-24. *Current* is the subject of the principal clause, and *glides* is the predicate.

62-2. *Book* is the direct and *sister* the indirect object of *gave.* Some grammarians would parse *sister,* and all similar constructions, as the object of the preposition *to* understood.

62-3. *To-day* is a noun in the objective case without a governing word expressed. Some authors supply the preposition; others parse such expressions as adverbs of time.

62-5. *Yourself* is in the nominative case, in apposition with *you.*

62-9. *On way* modifies *see.*

62-10. (To) *make* and (to) *compare* are objects of

dare, according to some authority; but the verb *dare* (venture) is not used in a transitive sense in this sentence. It is better to parse these infinitives as having the construction of adverbs, modifying *dare*. *Measuring* and *comparing* modify *they*.

62-11. *Country* is in the absolute case, and *land* is in apposition with *country*, or with *thee*. *It* is the subject, modified by the clause (that) *I sing*. Some authors claim that the clause, (that) *I sing*, is the subject of the sentence, and that *it* is an expletive. *Is of thee* is the predicate. The second *of thee* is an attendant element.

62-12. *Thou great Instructor* is a complex attendant element. *Instructor* is in apposition with *Thou*. *Feet* is the indirect object of *teach*, and *way* is the direct object.

68-3. *That* is the subject of *forsake*. *As* is a relative pronoun, and agrees with its antecedent *such*, or *persons* understood, in gender, person, and number; it is nominative to the verb *keep*. Some grammarians would parse *as* as a conjunction.

68-4. *There* is an expletive adverb. *Class* is the subject, and *is*, the predicate of the principal clause. *As* is a conjunctive adverb. *Those* belongs to *persons* understood, and *persons* understood is the object of the verb *dislike* understood.

69-6. *Whatever* is equivalent to *anything which*, or *that which*. The sentence may read, "Anything which is, is right;" or, "That which is, is right." Authors differ in their methods of parsing *whatever*. In following Harvey, we should parse the antecedent of *which* as nominative to the second *is*, and *which* as nominative to the first *is*.

69-7. Make the sentence read, "That which ye shall ask in my name, that will I do." The first *that* is in the absolute case by pleonasm; and *that which ye shall ask in my name* is a complex attendant element.

70-6. *Whom* is in the objective case after (not *of*) *to be*. Harvey says that a noun or pronoun following the infinitive *to be*, is in the same case as a word which precedes it.

70-9. *Lesson* is the subject, and *which* is the predicate.

70-10. *You* is the indirect, and *to parse* is the direct object of the verb *told*.

70-2. In the sentence, "I do not know *who* is in the garden," *who* is an interrogative pronoun, according to Harvey; but some authors would parse *who* as a relative, when used in this sense, agreeing with its antecedent understood; others would parse it as a responsive pronoun, because it is used in making replies to questions. The introduction of an antecedent converts an interrogative into a relative.

70-3. In the sentence, "Tell me *what* I should do," *what* may be parsed as an interrogative pronoun, object of *should do;* or as a double relative, equivalent to *the thing which*, or *the things which*.

71-7. *Which darkened the room* modifies the preceding clause.

71-4. *Worth* is a predicate adjective, and belongs to the subject *ounce*. *Ounces* is in the objective case without a governing word expressed; or the object of a preposition understood. Some authors would parse *worth* as a preposition, showing the relation between *ounces is*.

71-8. *Ye* understood is the subject. Some prefer to make *one* the subject. *One* m be parsed as an adjective used as a noun, nominative case in apposition with *ye*.

71-9. *More* is a noun, object of *could ask;* or it is an adjective, modifying *what*.

71-10. *Who* is the subject, and *is* is the predicate of the principal clause. *Base* is an adjective, and belongs to *who*. *So* is an adverb, modifying *base*. *That* is a conjunction, followed by *he* understood. The subordinate clause modifies *base;* or *so*, according to good authority. *Would be* is the copula, and *bondman* is the predicate.

71-11. The sentence is equivalent to *I speak as* (*I would speak*) *to wise men*. *As* is a conjunctive adverb. *As to* may be parsed as a complex preposition, unless the sentence be changed. *What* may be parsed as a double relative.

71-12. *Theirs* is a possessive pronoun, nominative case; or it may be parsed as a possessive pronoun, equivalent to *their right*. *As* is a conjunction, an index of apposition (Harvey); or a preposition (Holbrook). The first *men* is in the possessive case in apposition with *theirs*, or *their*, if the equivalent of *theirs* be given (Harvey). The second *men* is in the objective case after *to be* understood (See 70-6); or object of *did esteem*. (See Harvey's Grammar, page 154, remark 3).

71-13. *Philosophizing* is a present participle, and belongs to *Socrates*. *That could be desired* modifies the noun *death* understood.

71-14. *Popular Applause* is a proper noun, by personification; feminine gender, second person, singular number, absolute case.

71-15. The first *what* modifies *cares* understood; the second *what* modifies *cares*.

71-16. *Room* is the direct and *relics* the indirect object of *give*. *To slumber* modifies *room*.

71-17. *Spirit* is the direct object of (*to*) *share*. *Independence* is a proper noun of the masculine gender, second person, singular number; it is in the absolute case. *Lord* is in the absolute case, in apposition with *Independence*.

71-18. *On* is an adverb, modifying (*will*) *plod*. *As before* is equivalent to *as* (he did chase) *before*. *Before* is an adverb, modifying *did chase* understood. *As* is a conjunctive adverb. *Yet* is a conjunction.

81-1. *Tolling* is a present participle, and belongs to *bells*.

81-2. *Opened* is a perfect participle, and belongs to *letter*.

81-3. *Gambling* is a participial noun; it is neuter gender, third person, singular number, nominative case.

81-4. *Running, jumping* and *skating* are participial nouns, objects of the verb *like*.

82-6. *Having sold* is a compound participle, and belongs to *I*.

82-9. *Having been captured* belongs to *general*.

82-10. *Remaining* is a participial noun; it is the subject of the sentence.

82-11. *Said* and *marked* are perfect participles, and belong to *words*. *But* is an adverb, and modifies *once*. The second *but* modifies *softly*. *At all* is an adverbial phrase, modifying the participle *marked*.

82-12. *Hardened* belongs to *man*. *Complete*, an adjective, and *announced*, a participle, belong to *acquittal*.

82-13. *Washing* belongs to *ripple*, and *lapping* belongs to *water*.

82-14. *Toiling, rejoicing,* and *sorrowing* are present participles, and belong to *he*. *Attempted* belongs to *something*. The second *something* is in apposition with the first, and is modified by the participle *done*.

87-20. *Kingdom* is in apposition with *hell*.

88-21. *Save* is a preposition. *I* is used for *me* by poetic license. *Save the waves and I* (me) modifies *nothing*. Some authors would parse *save* as a subordinate conjunction, and *waves* and *I* as nominative to *may hear* understood.

112-1. *Plowing* is a participial noun, object of *commenced*.

112-6. *Should have been* is an irregular, copulative verb.

112-7. *Be hallowed* is a verb, regular, transitive, passive voice, imperative mode, present tense; it is of the third person, singular number, to agree with its subject *name*. (See page 86, remark 3).

112-9. *To do* is a verb, irregular, transitive, active voice, infinitive mode, present tense, and is the object of the verb *could learn*.

113-13. *Were mustered out* may be parsed as a complex transitive verb; or *out* may be parsed as an adverb.

113-19. The first two lines form a complex attendant element. *Law* is in the absolute case, by pleonasm. (To) *trickle* is in the infinitive mode, and depends upon *it*. The second *law* is nominative to *preserves* and *guides*. *Earth* and *sphere* are objects of *preserves*. (See page 154, remark 3). Some authors claim that *sphere* is in apposition with *earth ;* others would parse it as a noun in the objective case after *to be* understood.

113-21. *Wisest, brightest,* and *meanest* may be parsed as adjectives used as nouns, in apposition with *Bacon ;* or they may be considered adjectives, modifying *man* understood, which is in apposition with *Bacon.*

120-1. *Happily* is an adverb of manner, and modifies *lived. Very* is an adverb of degree, and modifies *happily.*

120-2. *Why* is an interrogative adverb, and modifies *do look. So* is an adverb of degree, and modifies *sad. Sad* is a predicate adjective.

120-3. *When* is a conjunctive adverb; it connects the two clauses, and modifies *comes.*

120-5. *Then* is an adverb of time, and *there* is an adverb of place; they modify *signed.*

120-6. *Again and again* is an adverbial phrase, and modifies *have read.*

120-7. *So* is an adverb of manner, and *no more* is an adverbial phrase, modifying the verb *will do.* The words forming the phrase may be parsed separately.

120-9. *Perchance* is an adverb of *manner* (Harvey); of *possibility* (Quackenbos); of *doubt* (Nash); it modifies *are.*

120-10. *Whither* is an interrogative adverb, and modifies *has gone.*

120-12. *Just* is an adverb, and modifies the phrase, *over the hill yonder,* or *over hill.*

120-13. *Henceforth* is an adverb of time; it modifies (to) *fear.*

120-14. *Before* is a conjunctive adverb; it modifies *left.*

120-15. *Not* is a modal adverb, modifying *will be.*

GRAMMAR. 69

120-16. *Not* modifies *have seen.* *Since* is a conjunctive adverb, modifying *returned.*

120-17. *Doubtless* modifies *are,* or *ye are the people.*

125-1. *With* shows the relation between *me* and *will go.* *Into* shows the relation between *garden* and *will go.*

125-2. *In* shows the relation between *house* and *are.* *Mansions* is the subject, and *are* is the predicate.

125-3. *Over* shows the relation between *river* and *went;* *through* between *corn-fields* and *went;* and *into* between *woods* and *went.*

125-4. *As to* is a complex preposition; it shows the relation between *affair* and *am satisfied.*

125-5. *But* shows the relation between *Mary* and *all.*

125-6. *From among* is a complex preposition; it shows the relation between *Alps* and *flows.* *Out* is an adverb, modifying *flows.*

125-9. *Aboard* shows the relation between *ship* and *went.*

125-10. *Goddess* is in apposition with *Night.* *From.* shows the relation between *throne* and *stretches.* *In* shows the relation between *majesty* and *stretches.* *Over* shows the relation between *world* and *stretches.* *Stretches forth* may be parsed as a complex verb; or *forth* may be parsed as an adverb, modifying *stretches.*

130-1. *And* is a coördinate conjunction; it connects *am* and *argue.* The second *and* connects *argue* and *convince.*

130-2. *Than* is a subordinate conjunction; it connects *sooner* and the subordinate clause. *Or* connects *you* and *man.*

130-3. *But* is a coördinate conjunction, and connects the two members.

130-4. *Neither* and *nor* are correlative conjunctions; *neither* introduces the sentence, and *nor* connects *military* and *civil*. Some authors claim that *nor* connects *pomp* and *pomp*.

131-5. *That* is a subordinate conjunction, introducing the predicate clause.

131-6. *But* is a coördinate conjunction, connecting the two members.

131-7. The adjectives, *alone, solitary,* and *idle,* belong to *I*. *And* connects *solitary* and *idle*.

131-8. *Both* and *and* are correlative conjunctions; *both* introduces the sentence, and *and* connects *ties* and *dictates*.

131-9. *There* is an expletive. *For* connects *was* and the subordinate clause.

131-10. *Than* is a subordinate conjunction; it joins the subordinate clause to *more;* or to *more highly*.

131-11. *On and on* is a complex adverb, modifying *marches*. *Inflicting* and *suffering* are present participles, and belong to *soldier*.

131-14. *As if* is a subordinate conjunction, and connects the two clauses.

131-17. *As to be hated,* etc., modifies *so;* or *frightful*. *She understood* is the subject of this subordinate clause, and *needs* is the predicate. *To be hated* is an adverbial element, and *to be seen* is an objective element, modifying *needs*. *But,* in the second line, is an adverb, modifying *to be seen*. The second couplet is equivalent to "We, familiar with her face, first endure, then pity, then embrace, (if she is) seen too oft." *Endure, pity,* and *embrace* form the compound predicate. *Familiar* is an adjective, and belongs to *we*. *Oft* modifies (is) *seen,* and *too* modifies *oft*.

133-4. *To freeze* limits *sight;* or it limits the subject *it.*
133-11. *What* and *farewell* are interjections. *Could keep in* is a complex verb; or *in* may be parsed as an adverb. *Life* is the object of the verb *could keep.*
133-3. *Far* is an adverb, modifying *beyond sea.*
133-6. *Ohs* and *ahs* are used as nouns; they are in the objective case.
133-8. *Union* is the antecedent of *which.*
134-11. The subordinate clause modifies *so.*
134-12. *But* shows the relation between *calm* and *joy.*
134-13. *To be kind* modifies *cruel. Only* modifies *to be kind. Kind* and *cruel* belong to *I.* Some authors claim that the phrase *to be kind* modifies *must be;* and that *only* modifies *kind.*
134-15. *All over* is an adverbial phrase, modifying *covers. Thoughts* and *all* are objects of *covers* understood. Some authors claim that these words are in apposition with *man.*
134-16. *Many a* belongs to *morning. Morning* is in the objective case without a governing word. (To) *ring* depends upon *copses.*
134-18. *As if* is a subordinate conjunction, and connects *acted* and the subordinate clause.
134-19. *Contention* is the subject, and *to find* is the predicate, of the first sentence. *Whilst* is a conjunctive adverb, and modifies *is living.* The clause, *Whilst an author is yet living,* modifies *estimate.*
134-20. *Other* belongs to *it. Other* is modified by *than it is.*
134-21. *So* and *as* are correlative conjunctions. *As* introduces the subordinate clause.

134-22. *Like* is a preposition, and shows the relation between *men* and *delighted*. Some authors would parse *like* as an adjective, belonging to *he ;* and *men* as the object of the preposition *to* understood.

134-23. *To know* is nominative to *is*. *To say* is the object of *to know*. *What* is a double relative pronoun. *Poets, sages, martyrs, reformers*, and *both* are in apposition with *men*. Some authors consider nouns of such construction as in the objective case after the infinitive copula *to be* understood.

134-24. *That done* is an abridged proposition, and modifies *turned* and *clung* (Irish); but some authors consider this phrase as an attendant element. *That* is in the absolute case with *done* or (being) *done*. *Done* belongs to *that*. *As* is a relative pronoun; its antecedent is *smile ;* it is the object of the two verbs, *had seen* and *could forget*.

134-25. *To live* is the subject, and *to die* is the predicate. *Behind* is an adverb, modifying *leave*. *Not* modifies *is*.

134-26. *But* is an introductory conjunction. *War* is nominative to *is*. *Which* is the object of *at*.

134-27. *Whoever* is equivalent to *he who ;* *he* is the subject of the second *thinks*, and *who* of the first *thinks*. *To see* is the object of *thinks*, and *piece* is the object of *to see*.

134-28. *Niobe* is in the absolute case by pleonasm. Some authors consider *Niobe* in apposition with *she*. *Childless* and *crownless* belong to *she*. Some authors consider *stands* the predicate ; others consider *stands* the copula, and *childless* and *crownless* predicate adjectives. *In her voiceless woe* modifies *she* (Irish); or *stands* (Adams); or *being* understood

(Eubank). *Urn* is nominative to *is* understood (Raub); or object of the participle *holding* understood (Irish); or in the absolute case with the participle *being* understood (Adams); or the object of *has* understood (Eubank). *Ago* modifies *was scattered*, and *long* modifies *ago*.

134–29. *Back* is an adverb, modifying *can call*. *Honor's* and *Death* are masculine, and *Flattery* is feminine gender.

135–30. *Owlet* is the subject, and *drops and holds* is the compound predicate, of the first member. *Atheism* is in apposition with *owlet*. *Sight* is in the absolute case by exclamation. *Sailing* is a present participle, and belongs to *owlet*. *Forth* (an adverb), *on wings*, *athwart noon*, *from hiding-place*, modify *sailing*. *Close* (closed) may be parsed as an adjective, belonging to *them*; or it may be parsed as an adverb, modifying *holds*. *He* understood is the subject, and *cries out* is the predicate, of the second member. *Out* may be parsed as an adverb. *Where is it* is the object of *cries out*, or of *cries*. *Hooting* belongs to *he* understood.

135–32. *Dry* is an adverb, modifying *clanked*. *Harness* is the subject of *clanked*. *All* (wholly) is an adverb, modifying the phrases *to left* and (to) *right*. Some authors consider *all* the subject of *clanged*; others consider it as an adverb, modifying *clanged*; others parse it as an adjective belonging to *cliff*. *Jets* is the antecedent of *that*. *Sharp-smitten* is a participle, modifying *that*. Some authors parse it as an adjective.

135–33. *Shadow* is the subject of *came wandering*, or of *came*. Some authors parse *wandering* as a participle in the predicate with *came*, belonging to *shadow*;

others parse it as an adverb modifying *came*. *Like* is a preposition, and shows the relation between *angel* and *shadow;* or it is an adjective, followed by the preposition *to* understood, and belongs to *shadow*. *With* shows the relation between *hair* and *angel*. *Dabbled* is a participle, and belongs to *hair*. *Out* and *aloud* are adverbs, modifying *shrieked*. The second word *Clarence* is in apposition with the first. *Is come* equals *has come*. *Furies* is a proper noun by personification; it is feminine gender, second person, absolute case by direct address.

135-34. *There* is an expletive in each of the first three lines. *Weak* is an adjective, belonging to *heart*. *Like* is a preposition, unless *comes* understood be supplied; it then becomes a conjunctive adverb.

135-35. *Record* is the object of *left;* and *columns, statues, ruins, streets,* and *cities* are in the same case by apposition. *Strown* is a participle, and belongs to *columns*. *Fallen, cleft,* and *heaped* are participles, and belong to *statues*. *Overthrown* is a participle, and belongs to *host*. The first *where* may be considered a conjunctive adverb joining its clause to *left;* or it may be parsed as a relative adverb (Raub), relating to *ruins*. An adjective clause is sometimes introduced by a relative adverb. The second *where* relates to *earth*. *Of* shows the relation of *air* to *breath*.

147-2. *Spread level* is equivalent to *was level; spread* is the copula, and *level* is the predicate.

147-4. *Lay* is the copula, and *dying* is the predicate.

147-6. *Ye and ye* is the compound subject of *descend* (Irish); or *ye* understood is the subject (Adams). Some authors parse *ye* in this sentence as an adjective; others consider it as a pronoun in the absolute case. *Dews* and *showers* should be parsed as appositives, unless *ye* is considered an adjective.

147-11. *All* modifies *village.*

147-13. *It* is an independent element, and the clause is the subject; or *it* may be called the subject, modified by the explanatory clause.

147-15. *Dares* is modified by (to) *touch,* and by *not,* adverbial elements.

147-19. *Till* is a preposition.

148-20. *But* modifies are; it is used in the sense of *only,* or *merely.*

148-22. *A hundred* modifies *souls; about* is an adverbial element, modifying *a hundred.*

148-24. The clause, *how the night behaved,* is the subject of some verb (*is, was,* or *did matter*). *What* modifies *matter,* as an adjective element; or *what* is an objective element, if *did matter* be used as the predicate. The second line is similar to the first in construction.

148-25. The clauses introduced by *where* modify *heaven. Bird* is an independent element.

163-1. *Behind thee* modiefis *crags.*

163-7. *Has become* is the copula.

164-3. *In snow* modifies *fresh.*

164-4. *Lay low* is equivalent to *was low, low* being a predicate adjective. *In valley* modifies *low.*

164-6. *Miles* is an adverbial element, modifying *ran.* A preposition is understood before *miles.*

165-3. *It* is the subject, and is modified by *to see;* or *it* is an independent element, and *to see* is the subject.

166-4. *It,* the subject, is modified by the clause,

who the old gentleman was; or *it* is an independent element, and the subordinate clause is the subject.

167-10. *At liberty* is the predicate, and is equivalent to *free*. *Now* and *to confess* are adverbialel ements, modifying *at liberty*. *Much* is the subject of *was founded*, and is modified by the subordinate clause introduced by *which*. *Objected* modifies *which*.

167-15. *Worth* is equivalent to *be*. The sentence is equivalent to *Woe be to the chase! woe be to the day!*

172-2. *Away* and *among shoulders* are adverbial elements, modifying *pursued*.

173-3. The clause, *that is not reason*, modifies *nothing*.

172-4. *Itself* modifies *Vice*. *Half* and *all* are objective elements. Some authors call them adjective elements in this sentence.

172-5. *There* is independent. *Limit* is the subject, and *is* is the predicate, of the principal clause. *Limit* is modified by the subordinate clause, *at which forbearance ceases to be a virtue*. *Ceases to be* is a strengthened copula. (See Harvey's Grammar, page 149). *To be* is an adverbial element, modifying *ceases*.

172-11. The clause introduced by *that* modifies *sure;* or it is an adjective element, modifying some noun understood, as *fact, truth*, etc.

173-15. *To be representative* modifies *which. Which* is the object of *found*.

174-9. The phrase introduced by *except* modifies *girls*. The clause beginning with *who* modifies *girls* understood.

174-10. The second word *tap* modifies the first, being in apposition with it.

180-18. The first line is equivalent to *Then here is*

(a toast) *to our boyhood*, (to) *its gold and* (to) *its gray.*
To is also understood before *stars* and *dews.*

189-22. The clause introduced by *that* modifies *it*. *At time, of family*, and the clause, *who probably imagines*, etc., modify *representative*. *In reality* modifies *is acting*. *Almost* is an adverbial element, modifying *every*.

189-24. *Seem to have been* is a strengthened copula, *seem* being modified by *to have been*, an adverbial element. *Like* is the predicate. *Boy* is the object of *to* understood. *Playing* and *diverting* are present participles, modifying *boy*. *Than ordinary* (pebbles are smooth or shells are pretty) modifies *smoother* and *prettier*. *Lay* is a copula. *All* equals *wholly*, and is an adverb, modifying *undiscovered*. *Before me* modifies *lay;* or it modifies *undiscovered*.

REMARK.—In some constructions it is difficult to decide upon the relation of the preposition, as in the foregoing sentence, in the use of *before*. There is ground for either view.

189-25. *Some* is an adjective element, modifying *we*. *Up* modifies *springing*.

189-27. The clause introduced by *where* modifies *seeks*.

189-30. *Rose* and *pillar* are predicates of the first member. *Seemed* is a copula. *Engraven* is an adjective used as the predicate after the copula *sat*.

190-31. *Near* is an adverb, modifying *rose;* and (to) *copse* modifies *near;* or *near copse* is a prepositional phrase, modifying *rose*.

Where once the garden smiled modifies *copse*. *Copse* is also modified by the next clause. *There* and the clause following modify *rose*. *Dear* and *rich* modify *man*. To *country* modifies *dear*. *Passing* is an adverbial element, modifying *rich*. *Rich* is also modified by *with pounds*. *Year*, or (in) *year*, is an adverbial element, modifying *forty*.

190-32. *Words* is the subject, and *came and went* is the compound predicate, of the principal clause. *Senators* is the subject, and *dream and dream* is the compound predicate, of the clause introduced by *those*. *Oaks* modifies *senators*, and *branch-charmed* modifies *oaks*. *So* modifies the second word *dream*. *Save from* is a complex preposition. *Off* is an adverbial element, modifying *dies*. *But* is an adverbial element, and modifies *one*. The second word *so* modifies *came* and *went*.

190-33. *She* is the subject, and *tore* and *set* is the compound predicate, of the principal clause. The predicate is modified by the clause, *when Freedom unfurled*, etc. *Unfurled* is modified by *standard*, an objective element; and by *when*, *from height*, and *to air*, adverbial elements. The second word *she* is the subject of *mingled*, and *striped*. *Baldric* is the object of *mingled*, and *white* is the object of *striped*.

NOTE.—Teachers and students desiring to purchase a book containing diagrams of most all the sentences in Harvey's English Grammar, are referred to Irish's "Grammar and Analysis Made Easy and Attractive by Diagrams," sold by the author, Frank V. Irish, A. M., Columbus, O. Those desiring a book containing a further and more elaborate discussion of the sentences in Harvey's English Grammar, are referred to "Hints and Helps on English Grammar," published by Raub & Co., Philadelphia.

Arithmetic.

SOLUTIONS

TO PROBLEMS FOUND IN RAY'S PRACTICAL ARITHMETIC.

Art. 82, problem 12.

$$\frac{124° \ \ 00'}{80 \ \ \ \ 42}$$

15) 43° 18' = difference of longitude.

2 hr. 53 min. 12 sec. = difference of time.

hr.	min.	sec.	
13	00	00	—hour at W.
2	53	12	

Ans. 10 hrs. 6 min. 48 sec. A. M.

Art. 130, problem 14.

$10000 ÷ 250 = 40, the number of lots.
150 ft. × 50 ft. = 7500 sq. ft., in one lot.
7500 sq. ft. × 40 = 300000 sq. ft., in 40 lots.
300000 sq. ft. ÷ 9 = 33333 sq. yd. +3 sq. ft.
33333 sq. yd. ÷ 30¼ = 1101 sq. rd. +27¾ sq. yd.
¾ sq. yd. × 9 = 27/4 sq. ft. = 6 sq. ft. +¾ sq. ft.
¾ sq. ft. × 144 = 108 sq. in.
6 sq. ft. + 3 sq. ft. = 9 sq. ft. = 1 sq. yd.
27 sq. yd. +1 sq. yd. = 28 sq. yd.
1101 sq. rd. ÷ 160 = 6 A. 141 sq. rd.
   Ans. 6 A. 141 sq. rd. 28 sq. yd. 108 sq. in.

Art. 160, problem 5.

49 m. 39.37 = 1929.13 in.
1929.13 in. ÷ 12 = 160 ft. 9.13 in.
160 ft. ÷ 3 = 53 yd. 1 ft.
53 yd. ÷ 5½ = 9 rd. 3½ yd.
½ yd. × 3 = 1½ ft. = 1 ft. 6 in.
9.13 in. + 6 in. = 15.13 in. = 1 ft. 3.13 in.
1 ft. + 1 ft. + 1 ft. + 3 ft. = 1 yd.
3 yd. + 1 yd. = 4 yd.
    Ans. 9 rd. 4 yd. 3.13 in.

Art. 169, problem 20.

$150 ÷ 1.25 = $120, the cost.
$200 — $120 = $80, the supposed gain.
$80 ÷ $120 = .66⅔ = 66⅔%, the rate. *Ans.*

Art. 173, problem 5.

100% = the list price.
10% = the first discount.
100% — 10% = 90%.
10% of 90% = 9%, the second discount.
90% — 9% = 81%.
10% of 81% = 8.1%, the third discount.
10% + 9% + 8.1% = 27.1%, sum of discounts.
$325.20 ÷ .271 = $1200, the cost of 20 dozens.
$1200 ÷ 20 = $60, the cost of one dozen. *Ans.*

Art. 174, problem 12.

$150 ÷ 1.25 = $120, cost of the first horse.
$150 ÷ .75 = $200, cost of the second horse.
$150 + $150 = $300, selling price of the two horses.
$200 + $120 = $320, cost price of the two horses.
$320 — $300 = $20, the loss. *Ans.*

ARITHMETIC.

Art. 175, problem 4.

12 × 3 = 36, the number of hats.
37½ cts. × 36 = $13.50, the whole profit.
$13.50 ÷ .125 = $108, the cost.
$108 ÷ .90 = $120, the list price. *Ans.*

Problem 5.

100 × 12 = 1200, the number of papers.
$1 × 100 = $100, the list price.
$100—$60 (first dis.) = $40.
$40—$2 (second dis.) = $38.
$38—1.90 (third dis.) = $36.10.
$36.10 — $23.90 — $60, the selling price.
$60 ÷ 1200 = 5 cts., the selling price of one paper. *Ans.*

Problem 7.

$125 × 80 = $10000, the cost of the horses.
$10000 + $200 = $10200, the cost and freight.
$10450 — $10200 = $250, the commission.
$250 ÷ 10000 = .025 = 2½%, the rate. *Ans.*

Problem 8.

1500 lbs. × 50 = 75000 lbs.
10½ cts. × 75000 = $7875.
$7875 × .02 = $157.50, the commission.
$157.50 + $22.50 (charges) = $180.
$7875 — $180 = $7695, the consignor receives.
$7695 ÷ 1.14 = $6750, the cost.
$6750 ÷ 75000 = 9 cts., the cost per pound. *Ans.*

Problem 10.

$35.91 ÷ 1.12 = $32.06¼, the cost.
$32.06¼ ÷ .95 = $33.75, third price.
$33.75 ÷ .90 = $37.50, second price.
$37.50 ÷ .75 = $50, first (list) price.
$50 ÷ 50 = $1, the list price per gross. *Ans.*

Art. 179, problem 10.

100%=the par value of the gold.
$\frac{1}{16}$%=15.62\frac{1}{2}$, the brokerage.
1%=15.62\frac{1}{2}$×16= $250.
100%=$250×100=$25000, the par value.
25731.37\frac{1}{2}$—$25000=734.37\frac{1}{2}$.
734.37\frac{1}{2}$+$15.62$\frac{1}{2}$=$750, premium.
$750÷25000=.03= 3%, rate of premium.
100%+3%=103%, the price of gold. *Ans.*

Art. 180, problem 5.

$5220÷1.16=$4500, amount in bonds.
$4500×.06=$270, annual income in gold.
$270×.05=$13.50, premium on the gold.
$270+$13.50= $283.50, income in currency. *Ans.*

Problem 6.

4$\frac{1}{2}$%= the income in gold.
5%=rate of premium on gold.
.045×.05=.00225=.225%, premium.
4.5%+.225%=4.725%, income in currency.
4.725÷1.08=4.375=4$\frac{3}{8}$%. *Ans.*

Problem 8.

$1921÷1.13=$1700, annual income in gold.
$1700÷.05=$34000, par value.
$34000×1.18=$40120, market value. *Ans.*

Problem 9.

95$\frac{1}{4}$+$\frac{1}{4}$= 95$\frac{1}{2}$, the cost, including the brokerage.
105—$\frac{1}{4}$=104$\frac{3}{4}$, the selling price, minus the brokerage.
104$\frac{3}{4}$—95$\frac{1}{2}$=9$\frac{1}{4}$%=.0925, the gain per cent.
$925÷.0925=$10000, amount of stock.
$10000÷100=100 shares. *Ans.*

Art. 191, problem 10.

$20000 = the value of the 20 bonds.
$4000 = the interest for 5 years.
$4000 ÷ 5 = $800, int. for 1 year.
$800 ÷ 4 = $200, int. for ¼ year.
¼ of 6% = 1½%, the rate per qr.
190. the number of qrs., (19+18- 17, etc.).
$3 = the int. on $200 for 1 qr.
$3 × 190 = $570, int. for 190 qrs.
$4000 + $570 = $4570, the income in gold.
$4570 × .05 = $228.50, gold premium.
$4570 + $228.50 = $4798.50, the income in currency. *Ans.*

Art. 197, problem 9.

	yr.	mon.	da.
	1877	1	4
	1876	2	19

10 mo. 15 da.

$0.014 = dis. on $1 for 2 mon. 24 da. at 6%.
$1 — $0.014 = $0.986, proceeds.
$1055.02 ÷ .986 = $1070, amt. for 10 mon. 15 da.
$0.07 = interest on $1 for 10 mon. 15 da. at 8%.
$1 + $0.07 = $1.07, am't of $1 for 10 mon. 15 da.
1070 ÷ 1.07 = $1000, the face of the note. *Ans.*

Art. 199, problem 15.

$2000 = the principal.
$ 292 = int. 1 yr. 9 mon. 27 da., at 8 %.

$2292 = the amt. due May 1, 1878.
$1.031 = amount of $1, 6 mon. 6 da., at 6 %.

$2292÷1.031 = $2223.08, present worth.
$2292—$2223.08=$68.92, the discount. *Ans.*

Art. 201, problem 6.

$1+$0.005=$1.005, rate of exchange.
$0.0105=the bank dis. of $1 for 63 days.
$1.005—$0.0105=$0.9945, cost of exchange for $1.
$5630×.9945=$5648.76, the cost. *Ans.*

Problem 7.

$1+$0.0075=$1.0075, rate of exchange.
$0.0055=bank dis. of $1 for 33 days.
$1.0075—$0.0055=$1.002, cost of ex. for $1.
$1575×1.002=$1578.15, the cost. *Ans.*

Problem 8.

$1+$0.015=$1.015, rate of exchange.
$0.0105=the bank dis. of $1 for 63 days.
$1.015—$0.0105=$1.0045, cost of ex. for $1.
$2625×1.0045=$2636.8125, the cost. *Ans.*

Art. 205, problem 7.

$29.15×6=$174.90, one annual premium.
$174.90×15=$2623.50, fifteen an. prems.
15+14+13+12+11 + 10 + 9 + 8 + 7 + 6 + 5 + 4 + 3 + 2 + 1 = 120 yr.
$174.90×.06×120 = $1259.28, the interest for 120 yrs.
$2623.50+$1259.28 = $3882.78, amt. paid out. *Ans.*

Art. 212, problem 4.

1317.04 m. + 34.36 m. = 1351.40 m.
1351.40 m.×.06 = 81.084 m., the commission.
1351.40 m.+81.084 m. = 1432.484 m., the total cost in marks.

ARITHMETIC. 85

1432.484 m.×23.8 (cts.)=$340.93, the total cost in dollars.
$341 (dutiable value) ×.25=$85.25, the duty. *Ans.*

Problem 5.

1500 ℔×50 (cts.)=$750.00, the *specific* duty.
£8 4s. 6 d.=£8$\frac{9}{40}$=£8.225, the charges.
£500+£8.225=£508.225, the cost and charges.
£508.225×.02$\frac{1}{2}$=£12.705+, the commission.
£508.225 + £12.705 = £520.93, the total cost in pounds.
£520.93×4.8665=$2535.11, the total cost in dollars.
$2535 (dutiable value)×.35=$887.25, the *ad valorem* duty.
$887.25+$750=$1637.25, the entire duty. *Ans.*

Art. 224, problem 33.

9 hr. : 12 hr. : : 15\frac{2}{3}$: what?=20.88\frac{8}{9}$.
20.88\frac{8}{9}$=worth of 1 mo.'s services, 12 hr. a day.
$ 20.88$\frac{8}{9}$×4$\frac{2}{5}$=91.91\frac{1}{9}$, worth of 4$\frac{2}{5}$ mo.'s services. *Ans.*

Problem 45.

70 p. : 20 p. : : 60 sec. : what?=17$\frac{1}{7}$ sec.
1142 ft.×17$\frac{1}{7}$=19577$\frac{1}{7}$ ft.=3 mi. 226 rd. 2 yd. 2$\frac{1}{7}$ ft. *Ans.*

Art. 225, problem 11.

100 men : 180 men
200 yd. l. : 180 yd. l.
3 yd. w. : 4 yd. w. } : : 6 days : what?=24.3 days.
2 yd. d. : 3 yd. d.   *Ans.*
8 hrs. : 10 hr.

Art. 229, problem 6.

$300 × 8 = $2400; $300 + $100 = $400; $400×8 = $3200; $3200+$2400= 5600, A's for 1 mo.

$600 \times 10 = \$6000$; $\$600 — \$300 = \$300$; $\$300 \times 6 = \$1800$; $\$1800 + \$6000 = \$7800$, B's for 1 mo.
$\$7800 + \$5600 = \$13400 =$ the whole for 1 mo.
$\frac{5600}{13400} = \frac{28}{67}$; $\$442.20 \times \frac{28}{67} = \$184.80$, A's.
$\frac{7800}{13400} = \frac{39}{67}$; $\$442.20 \times \frac{39}{67} = \$257.40$, B's.

Art. 231, problem 3.

Select July 6, when the first bill becomes due.
July   6, $1250×   00=000000
Sept. 17, $4280× 73=312440
Dec. 21, $ 675×168=113400

6205)   425840(69 da. nearly.
Counting 69 days from July 6, gives Sept. 13. *Ans.*

Art. 240, problem 4.

$60 \times 60 = 3600$; $37 \times 37 = 1369$; $3600 — 1369 = 2231$;
$\sqrt{2231} = 47.2334+$ ft. $=$ part width of street.
$60 \times 60 = 3600$; $23 \times 23 = 529$; $3600 — 529 = 3071$;
$\sqrt{3071} = 55.4166+$ ft. $=$ part width of street.
$47.2334+$ ft. $+ 55.4166+$ ft. $= 102.65 +$ ft. $=$ the entire width of the street. *Ans.*

Problem 5.

$600 \times 600 = 360000$; $140 \times 140 = 19600$; $360000 — 19600 = 340400$; $\sqrt{340400} = 583.43 +$ ft.; 100 ft. $\div 2 = 50$ ft.; $583.43 +$ ft. $— 50$ ft. $= 533.43 +$ ft., the breadth of the stream. *Ans.*

Problem 6.

$20 \times 20 = 400$; $16 \times 16 = 256$; $400 + 256 = 656$, the square of the diagonal of the floor, also of the base of the triangle, of which the hypotenuse is required.
$12 \times 12 = 144$; $656 + 144 = 800$; $\sqrt{800} = 28.28+$ ft. *Ans.*

ARITHMETIC. 87

Art. 252, problem 4.

10 ft.÷2=5 ft., the radius of the smaller circle; 16 ft.÷2=8 ft., the radius of the larger circle; 5×5×3.1416 =78.5400 sq. ft.=area of the smaller circle; 8×8× 3.1416=201.0624 sq ft.=area of the larger circle; 201.0624 sq. ft.—78.5400 sq. ft.=122.5224 sq. ft.; .5224 sq. ft.×144=75 sq. in. *Ans.* 122 sq. ft. 75 sq. in.

Art. 255, problem 3.

2+2+2=6; 6÷2=3; 3—2 = 1, first of three remainders.
3×1×1×1=3; $\sqrt{3}$=1.732+ sq. ft., area of base.
1.732+sq. ft.×14=24.248+cu. ft.= 24¼ cu. ft. nearly. *Ans.*

Art. 257, problem 4.

37⅔ ft.=$\frac{113}{3}$ ft.; $\frac{113}{3}$÷2=$\frac{113}{6}$; ($\frac{113}{6}$)²×3.1416 = 1114.3 -- sq. ft.=area of base; 1114.3+sq. ft ×(79¾÷3)=29622 +cu. ft. *Ans.*

Art. 259, problem 3.

1728÷5236 = 3300.229; $\sqrt[3]{3300.229}$ 14 9 in. nearly. *Ans.*

Art. 267, problem 4.

100=number of terms; 6=the first term, also the common difference.
100—1=99; 99×6=594; 594+6=600, the last term.
600 +6 = 606; 606×100=60600; 60600÷2 = 30300 yd.; 30300 yd.=17 mi. 69 rd. ½ yd. *Ans.*

Problem 5.

193 in. × 2 = 386 in., common difference; 386

$(60-1) = 22774$; $22774 - 193 = 22967$ in., the last term. $22967 + 193 = 23160$; $23160 \times 60 = 1389600$; $1389600 \div 2 = 634800$ in. 57900 ft. *Ans.*

ARITHMETICAL PROBLEMS.

1. $\frac{2}{3}$ of the difference between two numbers is 16; the smaller number is 12, what is the greater?
Ans. 36.

2. A has $\frac{3}{4}$ of $8560, which is $2\frac{1}{2}$ times B's money; how much money has B? *Ans.* $2568.

3. What is the smallest sum of money for which I could hire workmen for one month, paying either $30, $48, or $60 a month? *Ans.* $240.

4. On what sum of money is $100 the difference between the interest calculated at 4 per cent. per annum and that at $3\frac{1}{2}$ per cent. for every 10 months.
Ans. $50000.

5. $24 + 12 \times 13 - 3$ what? *Ans.* 177.
6. $24 - 12 \times (13-3) = $ what? *Ans.* 144.
7. $(24+12) \cdot 13 - 3 = $ what? *Ans.* 465.

REMARK.—The signs $\times$ and $\div$ cannot extend their power, forward or backward, beyond a $+$ or a $-$, without the aid of the parenthesis.

8. A has $2000; $\frac{3}{4}$ of his money $- $100 is $\frac{4}{7}$ of B's; what sum has B? *Ans.* $2800.

9. At what rate per cent. per annum will any sum of money double itself at simple interest in 30 years?
Ans. $3\frac{1}{3}$.

10. What number is that from which if we deduct $\frac{2}{7}$ of itself and $\frac{2}{5}$ of the remainder, there will be 23 left?
Ans. 63.

11. A man spent $\frac{2}{3}$ of $\frac{4}{5}$ more than half his money, and had $140 left; how much had he at first?
Ans. $600.

12. If the difference between two principals. which produce the same amount of interest, is $500, the one calculated at 4 per cent. and the other at 5 per cent., find the common interest. *Ans.* $100.

13. A loaned B $50 at 6 per cent. On payment B found that he was owing A just $75; how long did he use the money? *Ans.* 8 yr. 4 mo.

14. A man can row a boat down stream 12 miles per hour, and up stream 6 miles per hour; how far can he go down and return in 24 hours? *Ans.* 96 miles.

15. A man owning 40 per cent. of an iron foundry sold 25 per cent. of his share for $1246 50; what was the value of the foundry? *Ans.* $12465

16. A's money is 20 per cent. more than B's; then B's money is how many per cent. less than A's?
Ans. $16\frac{2}{3}$.

17. Bacon which costs 12 cents per pound wastes 15 per cent. before it is sold; at what price per pound must it be sold to gain 25 per cent? *Ans.* $17\frac{11}{17}$ cts.

18. A ladder 82 ft. long stands close against a building; how far must it be drawn out at the bottom that the top may be lowered 2 ft? *Ans.* 18 ft.

19. I spent 25 per cent. of my money, then 10 per cent. of the remainder, and had $567 left; what had I at first? *Ans.* 840.

20. Find the compound interest of $750 for 3 yr. 18 mo. 15 da., at 6 per cent., compounded annually.
Ans. 181.42.

21. Find the bank discount and proceeds of a note of $580 for 4 months, at 6 per cent.
Ans. $11.89 dis.; $488.21 proc.

22. What is the height of a tree which casts a shadow 36 ft. long, if a staff 8 ft. 6 in. cast a shadow 12 ft. 9 in.?
Ans. 24 ft.

23. If a 5-cent loaf weigh 12 oz. when flour is $4 a barrel, what should it weigh when flour is $6 a barrel?
Ans. 8 oz.

24. I sold a horse for $108, and lost 10 per cent.; for what would I have sold the horse to gain 10 per cent?
Ans. 132.

25. A wishes to borrow $2000 from a bank for 90 days; for what sum must he give his note, discounting at 6 per cent? *Ans.* $2031.50.

26. I invested $13200 in 7 per cent. stock, at 12 per cent. discount; what is my annual income?
Ans. $1050.

27. Find the simple interest on $6000 for 1 yr. 4 mo. 13 da., at 8 per cent. *Ans.* 657.33.

28. A cube has an area of 2400 sq. in.; find its solid contents. *Ans.* 8000 cu. in.

29. The principal is $400, the interest $137.60, and the time 4 yr. 3 mo. 18 da.; what is the rate?
Ans. 8 per. cent.

30. If $\frac{3}{4}$ of a farm is worth $1800, what is the value of $\frac{5}{6}$ of it? *Ans.* $2000.

31. A, B, and C dine on 8 loaves of bread; A furnishes 5 and B 3; C pays them 18 cents; how should A and B divide the money? *Ans.* A 15¾c., B2¼c.

32. In what time will $126.50 give $2.53 interest at 5 per cent? *Ans.* 4 mo. 24 da.

33. Find the asking price of a hat, which cost $1.20,

so as to abate 6¼ per cent., and still make a profit of 25 per cent. *Ans.* $1.60.

34. 100 eggs are placed in a right line, exactly 2 yards apart, the first being 2 yards from a basket; how far will a man travel who gathers them up singly, and places them in the basket? *Ans.* 11 mi. 152 rd. 4 yd.

35. A window sill is just 40 feet from the ground; how far from the wall of the house must a ladder 50 feet long be placed to reach the sill? *Ans* 30 ft.

36. Find the diagonal of a room 40 feet long, 30 feet wide, 12 feet high. *Ans.* 51. 4÷ft.

37. How large a square can be cut out of a circular board whose circumference is 100 inches?
Ans. 22. 5÷in.

38. How many feet of lumber in 21 planks, each 16 feet long, 18 inches wide, and 2 inches thick?
Ans. 1008 ft.

39. Two principals produce the same annual interest, $100, one at 4 per cent., the other at 5 per cent.; find the difference of the principals. *Ans.* $500.

40. Divide 1272 by the square root of 2809.
Ans. 24.

41. Divide the square root of 57600 by the cube root of 512, and multiply the quotient by the cube of 4.
Ans. 1920.

42. A sphere is 4 feet in diameter; find its contents.
Ans. 33.5104 cu. ft.

43. The area of a circle is 490.875 square feet; what is the diameter? *Ans.* 25.

44. If a ball 3 inches in diameter weigh 9 pounds, what is the weight of a ball 4 inches in diameter?
Ans. 21⅓ lb.

45. Compare the areas of two circles whose diameters are as 4 : 6. *Ans.* 16 : 36.

46. I bought a horse for $70 cash, and sold him for $84, at a credit of 10 months; reckoning the interest at 6 per cent., how much did I gain. *Ans.* $10.

47. The boundaries of a square and circle are each 64 feet; find the difference between the areas.
Ans. 69.93 sq. ft.

48. Find the solid contents of a cone, diameter of base being 20 feet, altitude 30 feet.
Ans. 3141.6 cu. ft.

49. A cubical cistern holds 200 gallons; what is its depth? *Ans.* 35 in.

50. The solidity of a sphere is 33.5104 cu. ft.; what is the diameter? *Ans.* 4 ft.

51. Find the cost of fencing a square lot, containing 160 acres, at the rate of $4 per rod. *Ans.* $2560.

52. A general wishes to place 7225 men in the form of a square; how many must he put in each line?
Ans. 85.

53. Find the area of a triangle whose sides are 16, 18, and 20 feet. *Ans.* 136+ sq. ft.

54. A ladder 130 feet long will reach to a window 78 feet high on one side of a street, and on the other to a window 50 feet high; find the width of the street.
Ans. 224 ft.

A BRIEF CHRONOLOGY OF GENERAL HISTORY.

Asia.

B. C.

4004. The Creation of the world.
2348. The Great Deluge covers the earth.
2247. The Confusion of Tongues.
888. The first Assyrian empire overthrown.
606. The second Assyrian empire overthrown.
538. The overthrow of the Babylonian empire.
536. Cyrus the Great establishes the Persian empire.
480. Leonidas defeated by Xerxes.
312. The kingdom of Syria founded by Seleucus.
67. Chang becomes emperor of China.
61. The Romans conquer Syria and Canaan.

A. D.

0. Birth of Christ; the beginning of the Christian Era.
33. Christ crucified.
70. Titus destroys Jerusalem.
570. Birth of Mohammed.
638. The Saracen empire established.
1253. The Saracen empire overthrown by the Turks.
1400. Japan discovered by Europeans.
1854. Treaty between the United States and Japan.

Africa.

B. C.

2188. Egypt settled by Misraim.
1491. The Israelites depart from Egypt.
525. Cambyses conquers Egypt.

520. Thebes destroyed by Cambyses.
332. Alexander conquers Egypt.
30. Death of Cleopatra.

A. D.

670. Egypt conquered by the Saracens.
1517. The Turks conquer Egypt.
1798. Napoleon invades Egypt.
1815. Commodore Decatur attacks Algiers.
1876—1877. Henry M. Stanley crosses the continent.

Europe.

B. C.

1856. Greece founded by Inachus.
1556. Athens founded by Cecrops.
1500. Thebes founded by Cadmus.
752. Rome founded by Romulus.
500. The Carthaginians make conquests in Spain.
446. Peloponnesian War begins.
396. The Gauls ravage Italy, and take Rome.
323. Death of Alexander, king of Macedon.
264. First Punic War begins.
218. Second Punic War begins.
206. The Romans conquer Spain.
149. Third Punic War.
146. Greece reduced to a Roman province.
91. Social War in Greece begins.
59. First Triumvirate formed in Rome.
58. France invaded by Julius Cæsar.
55. Britain invaded by Julius Cæsar.
44. Cæsar assassinated.
43. Second Triumvirate; death of Cicero.
25. The Romans complete the conquest of France.

A. D.

14. Death of Augustus Cæsar, emperor of Rome.

44. England subdued by the Romans.
60. Christianity introduced into England.
290. The Romans expelled from Germany.
395. Rome divided into the Eastern and Western empire.
400. France invaded by Germanic tribes.
410. Rome taken by Alaric, a barbaric leader.
476. Rome taken by Odoacer, chief of the Goths.
827. Egbert I. becomes king of England.
871. Alfred ascends the English throne.
877. England conquered by the Danes.
1041. Danes expelled from England.
1066. Harold ascends the throne of England.
1096. First Crusade begun, led by Peter the Hermit.
1139. Kingdom of Portugal founded.
1215. Magna Charta granted by King John.
1248. Last Crusade begun.
1299. Ottoman empire founded.
1328. Beginning of the Hundred-Years War.
1330. Gunpowder first used in war. It was probably invented by Roger Bacon, an English monk of the 13th century, and first applied to war, by a German named Schwartz.
1438. Printing by means of movable types of wood invented by a Dutch mechanic named Koster.
1441. Printing by means of movable types of metal invented by John Gutenberg, a German.
1455. Wars of York and Lancaster begun.
1456. First edition of the Bible printed. It was printed in the Latin language, by Gutenberg.
1517. Reformation commenced by Martin Luther.
1558. Elizabeth becomes queen of England.
1581. The republic of Holland founded.

1642. Civil war in England begun.
1649. Charles I. of England beheaded.
1654. Cromwell made Lord Protector of England.
1660. Charles II. becomes king of England.
1760. George III. ascends the English throne.
1798. Switzerland conquered by the French.
1804. Napoleon made emperor of France.
1809. War between France and Austria.
1815. Battle of Waterloo—Napoleon overthrown.
1824. Death of Lord Byron.
1837. Victoria becomes queen of England.
1848. Revolution in France, and the country becomes a republic.
1851. Republican government in France terminated by Louis Napoleon.
1852. Louis Napoleon becomes emperor of France.
1870. Franco-Prussian War; Napoleon overthrown—a republic established.
1874. Alfonso XII. becomes king of Spain.
1877. The Turko-Russian War begins.
1882. Death of Gambetta, of France.
1891. Death of Charles Stewart Parnell.
1892. Death of Lord Alfred Tennyson, Poet Laureate of England.

Prepare!

To do business intelligently and with a rush at the NATIONAL PEN ART HALL AND BUSINESS COLLEGE, Delaware, O.

All departments are headed by teachers of experience. More graduates holding good positions than any other college in the U. S.

Send for Catalogue and Advocate.

Address,

G. W. MICHAEL,
DELAWARE, O.

www.ingramcontent.com/pod-product-compliance
Lightning Source LLC
Chambersburg PA
CBHW021949160426
43195CB00011B/1284